AF800598

Is Capitalism Still Progressive?

"In his wide-ranging analysis of the history and perspectives of capitalism, Cosimo Perrotta displays at their best the pessimism of the intellect and the optimism of the will. Capitalism is a difficult beast, with many different varieties: a humane, civil capitalism requires complex strategies of intervention, and Perrotta's proposals deserve our full attention."

—Alessandro Roncaglia, *Professor of Economics, University of Roma "La Sapienza"*

Cosimo Perrotta

Is Capitalism Still Progressive?

A Historical Approach

palgrave
macmillan

Cosimo Perrotta
University of Salento
Lecce, Italy

ISBN 978-3-030-48168-1 ISBN 978-3-030-48169-8 (eBook)
https://doi.org/10.1007/978-3-030-48169-8

© The Editor(s) (if applicable) and The Author(s), under exclusive licence to Springer Nature Switzerland AG 2020
This work is subject to copyright. All rights are solely and exclusively licensed by the Publisher, whether the whole or part of the material is concerned, specifically the rights of translation, reprinting, reuse of illustrations, recitation, broadcasting, reproduction on microfilms or in any other physical way, and transmission or information storage and retrieval, electronic adaptation, computer software, or by similar or dissimilar methodology now known or hereafter developed.
The use of general descriptive names, registered names, trademarks, service marks, etc. in this publication does not imply, even in the absence of a specific statement, that such names are exempt from the relevant protective laws and regulations and therefore free for general use.
The publisher, the authors and the editors are safe to assume that the advice and information in this book are believed to be true and accurate at the date of publication. Neither the publisher nor the authors or the editors give a warranty, expressed or implied, with respect to the material contained herein or for any errors or omissions that may have been made. The publisher remains neutral with regard to jurisdictional claims in published maps and institutional affiliations.

Cover pattern © Melisa Hasan

This Palgrave Pivot imprint is published by the registered company Springer Nature Switzerland AG.
The registered company address is: Gewerbestrasse 11, 6330 Cham, Switzerland

To the slave children of the twenty-first century

Contents

Introduction

A Farewell to Capitalism?

This book is not about the end of capitalism, although many authors would now like to see it.[1] Leaving aside the countless guises capitalism has taken on in the course of history, in the strict sense it consists in a steady process of investment of wealth with the aim of generating further wealth in the form of profit. Such investments are typically the result of free choices by individuals motivated by personal interest in enrichment.

Capitalism is different from any other economic system insofar as it has led to a steadily growing production of wealth. It has thus come to represent a radical advance in human evolution, opening the way for the development of individuals' faculties that had previously found little scope if indeed any—individual initiative, the desire for enrichment, and the desire to see one's merits recognised.

So far there has been only one, tragic attempt to move on from capitalism, inspired by the socialist ideal of eliminating the grave injustices of economic exploitation. But the so-called real socialism eventually proved economically non-viable, with productivity tending towards zero. And even before economic failure came social failure since, from the very outset, it took the form of a monstrous system of oppression and violence, although this was the exact opposite of what it aimed at. This failure shows that personal interest cannot give way forever to dedication to a collective ideal.

[1] See Sivini (2016), offering in-depth analysis of the various theories on the end of capitalism.

This was all the more the case in a context that saw the (inevitable) formation of a new, privileged élite, in stark contrast with the egalitarian inspiration.

This is certainly not to justify the perverse tendency of capitalistic accumulation to exploit and oppress with no limits. It is, however, a tendency that can be curbed by means of the very same freedom that wealth opens the way to. On the strength of the well-being created by capitalism, people—some, if not all—have the possibility to grow culturally, defend themselves from the powerful and limit the injustices generated by the pursuit of profit. Other systems, where poverty dominates the less privileged classes, do not offer the resources to fight oppression. The poor societies are always oppressive.

This does not mean that it is right to defend the contemporary neoliberalism. For example, Iversen and Soskice endorse today's "advanced capitalism" as "embedded knowledge-based liberalism". This capitalism, they claim, is creating a "knowledge-based society" in which the vast majority get rich.[2] The authors deny that neoliberalist policy has expropriated the majority of economic agents. On the contrary, they see it as the result of decisions taken in full awareness by the majority and of widespread processes of technical and professional enhancement. This book shows a different picture; the virtuous process of the welfare state was moving in that direction but stopped all too soon, as particular and corporative interests came to prevail over the general interest.

> The authors arguing that the course of history is marked by diminishing violence seem decidedly optimistic (although Pinker is more wary on the subject).[3] On the basis of the data—for example, on the differences between the Middle Ages and the present day, or between the stateless populations and our states—there does appear to have been a quantitative reduction of private violence, for which we might also credit capitalism and the wealth it has produced. But these data do not tell the whole story. The genocides of the twentieth century, and the Shoah in particular evidenced unprecedented human degradation. The twentieth century also saw tens of millions slain through wars and ideological conflicts.[4]

[2] See Iversen and Soskice (2019), and in particular Chap. 4.

[3] Pinker (2011, e.g.: 692–96).

[4] Ibid.: 337.

Nor does the cyclical view do justice to capitalism. A hefty study by Van Bavel (2016) analyses various cases of development in a number of different areas before and during the rise of capitalism, when élites formed and concentrated the wealth which they then turned into means of political power. In the long run, the predominance of élites ossifies the institutions and brings the factors of production to act no longer as drivers of development but as factors of stagnation. The author sees the present crisis, too, as a sign of inevitable decadence. However, a number of simple facts seem to contradict this thesis, including the growth of China and many African countries, the growth of the digital economy and human capital, and the commitment of Europe to a new—green and immaterial—economy.

On the other hand, Milanovic (2017) criticises the idea of the circular economy (or doughnut economy),[5] pointing out the need for growth. Static societies, he argues, even when they are rich, eventually create discontent since simply making do with what one has is alien to human nature, and can never last for long. And yet Milanovic fails to take into account the fact that the desire for more and more does not necessarily focus on material goods. Beyond a certain level of material well-being, most individuals feel the need for cultural enrichment—more freedom, or more creativity—with no wish to dominate others through increasing self-enrichment at the material level.

At the other extreme, J.S. Mill, Keynes and, in his own way, Marx, too, believed that once the needs of all had been satisfied, society would reach a state of quiet contentment, a stationary state. Individuals would no longer be jostling for success.[6] All would have repudiated the *auri sacra fames*—the wretched greed for gold—as Virgil put it. But these great authors ignored the fact that there will always be a minority engaged in relentless pursuit of enrichment. The urge may be contained and controlled, but it would be extremely dangerous in terms of social freedom to seek to suppress it, as Keynes himself admitted.[7] Essentially, even the theoreticians of the stationary state conceived of economic wealth solely as a collection of material goods. But cultural enrichment has no limits, and can grow indefinitely.

The exponents of the circular economy make the same mistake of limiting the concept of wealth to material goods. They are worried about the

[5] On which see Raworth (2017).

[6] J.S. Mill (1848, IV.6.3–9). Marx (1863–1883, *Capital III*, VII.XLVIII.13). Keynes (1930).

[7] Keynes (1936, 24.I).

environmental damage that uncontrolled consumption of resources is causing. Hence the need to limit repetitive consumption and systematically recycle the materials consumed. However, if we fail to smooth transition to primarily cultural consumption we will find ourselves falling back on the utopia of the stationary state.

The protagonist of cultural consumption is human capital, whose growth is a combination of motive power and the effect of capitalistic accumulation over the last 150 years. The growth of human capital does not lie solely in immaterial production (such as research, education, training, organisation, culture, art and so on). It also leads to discovering new uses of materials, new materials and new resource-saving techniques. But to achieve all this, priority must return to the general interest, albeit leaving the due room for private interests.

* * *

I am very grateful to Alessandro Roncaglia, Estrella Trincado, Salvatore Rizzello, Mario Pianta, André Tiran and Claudia Sunna for their helpful suggestions and indeed for pointing out some errors. I also owe thanks to my son Paolo and his wife Maria Irene Sulpizio for having directed me to some valuable sources of data; Graham Sells for his sound work on the English text; and the friends and relations who encouraged me in this task. Of course, I have sole responsibility for any mistakes there may be. For the various texts and publications cited in the References and notes, I went straight to the sources (for them and for many others).

C.P., 15 January, 2020

References

Iversen, T., & Soskice, D. (2019). *Democracy and Prosperity.* Princeton and Oxford: Princeton U.P., e.book.

Keynes, J. M. (1930). Economic Possibilities for Our Grandchildren. In *Essays in Persuasion*, pp. 358–373. New York: Norton, 1963, online (yale.edu).

———. (1936). *The General Theory of Employment, Interest and Money.* London: Macmillan, 1973.

Marx, K. *Capital III.* (1863–1883). Trans. from German, First Ed. 1894. New York: International Publishers, online: marxists.org, 1999.

Milanovic, B. (2017, July 12). Inevitability of the Need for Economic Growth.... *Globalinequality*, blog.

Mill, J. S. (1848) *Principles of Political Economy with Some of Their Applications to Social Philosophy*, 7th ed. London: Longmans & Green, 1909, online Library of Economics & Liberty.

Pinker, S. (2011). *The Better Angels of Our Nature. A History of violence and Humanity.* Penguin.

Raworth, K. (2017). *Doughnut Economics.* London: Random House, 2018.

Sivini, G. (2016). *La fine del capitalismo. Dieci scenari.* Trieste: Asterios.

Van Bavel, B. (2016). *The Invisible Hand? How Market Economies have Emerged and Declined Since A D 500.* Oxford: Oxford U. P.

CHAPTER 1

Capitalism Creates Progress

Abstract Pre-capitalist systems are dominated by unproductive rent; the production of wealth is static and society is poor. Usually, these are agricultural societies with backward production processes. The systems may take the form of feudal-type regimes characterised by latifundia, or regimes with centralised economic power like China or the Ottoman Empire. Only capitalism owes its existence to the free initiative of individuals, and it generates a continual increase in wealth. The culture of capitalism derives from the rational, critical attitude of Western thought, and in some cases even from conflict between political and religious powers, which prevented any absolute authority from forming. The economic and social data show the historical progress of capitalistic societies.

Keywords Pre-capitalist systems • Rent • Feudal economy • Landowners • Free initiative

1.1 Pre-capitalist Systems and the Reign of Rent

1.1.1 Why Capitalism is Better than Other Systems

All the non-capitalist economic systems lack the essential requisites that are characteristic of capitalist accumulation, including: the freedom to choose one's own work and enrich oneself; the productive use of profit, which is largely reinvested to obtain further profit; continual increase in

© The Author(s) 2020

C. Perrotta, *Is Capitalism Still Progressive?*,
https://doi.org/10.1007/978-3-030-48169-8_1

the division of labour, which has generated the differentiation of crafts and professions and the growth of the middle classes. These primary characteristics have in turn given rise to continuous growth in productivity and wealth, competition amongst individuals and impersonal selection of the most able as well as, in the course of time, social mobility, protection of individual rights, the guarantees of the law and freedom of speech and association.

In general the pre-capitalist systems distribute the tasks of labour amongst the various social classes, supervise their work, and at the same time exploit the poor and guarantee their survival. These systems are essentially dualistic: there is a ruling elite, controlling the production and distribution of wealth, and a mass of poorer classes which produce the wealth. The division of labour has not progressed very far amongst them, and there is scant room for individual initiative or economic freedom. Wealth tends to reproduce consistently in the same quantities (it is a simple reproduction system, as Marx put it). Thus the social structures also tend to reproduce with few changes. There is no social mobility, with some exceptions for the religious and for intellectuals. Selection of the most able is based on co-optation, and is therefore often random and arbitrary.

While these systems are static, capitalism is dynamic, but precisely for this reason it is more exposed to imbalances and failures. Thanks to capitalistic accumulation it has been possible to move on from mainly agricultural to artisan and commercial production (this stage is also common to other civilisations), and thus on to manufacture, industry and, finally, the post-industrial economy where immaterial production and the growth of human capital predominate.

The systems closest in time to capitalism are of two types: feudal, or at any rate based on latifundia, where power is concentrated mainly in the hands of the landowners, and highly centralised systems in which the elite is represented by the governing class.

1.1.2 The Feudal Economy and the Latifundium

Capitalism was born within European feudalism, but fighting the system. The feudal economy, which is to be found in many historical contexts, rests on the labour of the peasants, bound in various ways to the land (serfs), with obligatory corvée (unpaid work for the feudal lord or the government). The feudal economy is poor, based on rent and hoarding, not on profit.[1]

Often feudalism sets in because the central powers have difficulty in directly administrating vast areas, and the sovereign assigns portions of land to the trusted few to manage.[2] In the system there is no clear-cut distinction between private and public property. The feudal lord is both owner and political master, oppressing the peasants but with the duty to protect and govern them. The feud is often hereditary.[3]

Feudalism is a form of latifundium, concentrating a large part of the land in the hands of a few families. In some cases the latifundium precedes and gives rise to the feudal structure. For example, in ancient Rome between the first and second century BC, the landowners among the noble families acquired vast quantities of slaves or servants (war spoils or ruined peasants) and monopolised agricultural production for export. The revenues were invested in the purchase of yet more land, for when agriculture is based on primitive techniques the proportion of rent depends essentially upon the dimensions of the estate; the outlay is minimal because exploitation of the land is very limited and cultivation extensive.

In other cases, the latifundium derives from the feudal system but outlasts its crisis. In south-east Germany and the whole of Eastern Europe latifundia expanded in the modern age due to the growing demand for foodstuffs in Western Europe (going through a phase of development). In Russia serfdom was abolished only in 1861, but this was not followed by effective liberation of the peasants.[4] In southern Italy the feudal system was abolished in 1806–1808 by the Napoleonic sovereigns, but the big landowners succeeded in piecing together the latifundia once again, driving the peasants' farms to failure.[5] Crisis came for the latifundia only in the 1950s, due to agrarian reform and, above all, large-scale emigration. In Portugal and Spain, the dominance of latifundia began to crumble when the countries opened up to the international economy.

Outside Europe, in the twentieth century the concentration of land in the hands of a few hundred owners still covered something between 70% and 90% of the total. Agrarian reform came to Ethiopia in 1975. In the

[1] See Cavalli (1974, ch. II).
[2] Brentano (1923: 14–15).
[3] Weber (1919–20, I.3–4: 48–63).
[4] Bevilacqua (1996: 168, 170).
[5] Cutrona (2012: 95–97).

rest of sub-Saharan Africa, as indeed in Iraq (where 1% of the population possessed 70% of the land), India, Pakistan and Indonesia the latifundium system had been reinforced under European colonisation, which often destroyed the old community economy of the villages.[6] In China the system was hit by crisis only with the victory of Mao (in 1949). In the colonial countries latifundia began to crumble after the various wars of liberation in the 1960s.

In Japan the feudal system lasted for many centuries. Solidly organised and run by the great feudal lords, it was based on the military class of the samurai together with the central administration of the court nobles. Abolition, in 1871, saw the beginning of a process of reform and modernisation which came up against the opposition of the samurai with a series of revolts, but was guided by the central government acting in the name of the Emperor. Nevertheless, it took some time for the economic enterprises to be placed entirely in private hands. By the end of the century the feudal system had disappeared.[7]

In India the existence of large-scale landed property was attested as early as the second millennium BC. The warrior caste (Ksatriya)—the second after the Brahmins—represented the landowners who used slaves or waged workers bound to the land (Sudra) for work in the fields. From the eighteenth century BC to the tenth century AD the north of India was characterised by a feudal structure; after the year 1000 it was to be found in Rajasthan and central India. In the other regions of India there were village communities or centralised administration. Entrusting the uncultivated land to the tax collectors, who held hereditary appointments, the British created a new class of landowners faithful to the British Crown. The old landowning nobility was marginalised, but later power was restored to the maharajas to curb the anti-British revolts.[8] At the time of independence there was still a very high concentration of land ownership; 5% of the families possessed 41% of the land and the poorest 61% were left with only 8% of it.[9]

In Mexico crisis hit the feudal type of *hacienda* after the revolution of 1910, but it has yet to disappear. In Argentina, latifundia remained in many areas, transforming into enterprise for the production and export of

[6] Borsa (1977, ch. III.2–3).
[7] Borsa (1977, ch. VII).
[8] Tinker (1983: 347–351, passim).
[9] Sideri (2010: 79).

meat. According to UNO, in the whole of Latin America in 1960 108,000 landowners possessed 65% of the private land, with an average of 4300 hectares each.[10] Basically, throughout America the latifundia introduced by the Spanish and Portuguese conquistadors resisted all attempts at reform.

In the feudal and latifundium systems there has always been a huge gap between the rents of the feudal lord/landowner and those of the peasants and artisans. Yet even more important was the difference in power. Adam Smith wrote that the European feudal lords consumed their rents not so much to possess luxury goods as to keep a great number of servants and armed men and show off their power.[11] Often abolition of the formal feudal bond not only failed to improve but actually worsened the conditions of the lower classes. The landowners, released from the obligation to defend the population and guarantee their survival, were able to exploit even more intensively the peasants who were eternally indebted to them and had no chance of changing work.

In some cases, however, the latifundium served to embark upon capitalistic investment, transforming into a proactive modern farm, as in the case of Argentina and Austria in the twentieth century. Max Weber describes this process in eastern Germany, Poland and Russia in the nineteenth century.[12] In the United Kingdom resort to enclosures (abusively privatising common land) became particularly intensive in the fifteenth to sixteenth and eighteenth to nineteenth centuries, which saw capitalistic development accelerating thanks to wool production in the former period and industrial cotton production in the latter.

In many regions long dominated by the feudal or latifundium structure (Ireland, South Italy, Eastern Europe, Latin America, India, the Middle East and Southeast Asia) traces of the old systems are still fairly evident even today. For example, the wealthy are traditionally attributed with particular privileges. In these cases, favouritism and abuse prevail over merit and competition, and investment tends to transform into rent. These regions are characterised by weak democracy, paternalism and scant transparency. The most serious shortcoming lies in the cultural and numerical weakness of the middle classes, which have a share in some of the privileges of the wealthy and look more to rent than to profit.

[10] Bevilacqua (1996: 169, 172–173).
[11] Smith (1776, V.III, first paragraph).
[12] Weber (1919–20, I.6: 71–76).

1.1.3 The Centralised Systems

In other systems the latifundium has played a secondary role, but capitalism failed to set in nevertheless, society remaining dualistic. In China, after a feudal-type phase, with the great landowners ever at war against one another (the age of the warlords, eighth to fourth century BC), direct relations became established between the sovereign and the peasants. In the third century BC the great landowners were actually expropriated and exiled. A class of bureaucrats (the Mandarins) emerged; selected by competitive examination, they came from the minor landowning nobility, controlled the local administrations on behalf of the Emperor and were substitutable.[13] Subsequently, the sovereign had to accept the re-emergence of a class of agrarian nobles, but they would never again enjoy political power.

Merchants, however, had no access to the competitive examinations to become Mandarins. Consequently, as Schefold observes, the state failed to introduce the credit system and contract law—as established in Europe—without which commerce was thwarted and left on the sidelines of the economy.[14] This prevented China from generating capitalism, despite having been technically more advanced than Europe for many centuries.

It was precisely when Europe was approaching the transition to capitalism that China saw a period of extraordinary economic and social development under the two Song dynasties, the northern dynasty (960–1127) and the southern one (1127–1279). The technical inventions then achieved in China range from the printing press with movable type to gunpowder, paper money and the compass. Striking development was also achieved in the iron and arms industries; the shipyards, with a great merchant fleet; and the production of porcelain, silk and velvet. Wood was replaced by coal as fuel for the production of cast-iron. Private enterprises worked alongside those of the state. The artisan and merchant corporations fixed wages and prices, as in Europe. In the twelfth century, a little ahead of Florence and Flanders, China saw the construction of great factories with hundreds of waged workmen.

The Yuan (1279–1368) and Ming (1368–1644) dynasties saw yet further development. Schools were set up in every province; a great flow of trade emerged involving the Islamic merchants of eastern Asia. The arts

[13] See Breuer (1994: 532).

[14] Schefold (2019: 20–21).

and literature flourished, while the seventeenth century saw the adoption of smallpox vaccine a hundred years before Jenner. Agriculture and canalisation of the water resources were taken yet further in the eighteenth century; it was a time of great demographic growth, while both the administrative and fiscal systems were reorganised. A petty bourgeoisie grew up in the cities, and slavery was actually abolished.[15]

Again, the Song dynasties saw consolidation of the practice of state exams to select the Mandarins, who were rather like the English gentry, although the latter succeeded in utilising the latifundia of the feudal lords to make investments for profit and creating conditions for the take-off of British capitalism. By contrast, the Chinese functionaries-scholars, faithful to the rules of Confucius, governed the people with a paternalistic approach, adopting measures (with the public granaries) to overcome famine and flooding; they worked "for the well-being of the people", but were defined by Billeter as "one of the most exploitative classes in history".[16]

Moreover, it was again in the Song period that the Chinese peasants turned into sharecroppers and became subject to corvées to create dams and canals. Women lost their previous status; they now had to have their feet bound and accept their husbands' concubines.[17] Craft and industrial trades were subordinated to the requirements of agrarian rent. Gradually Chinese society came to a halt, dominated by the farmers. It was the same ineluctable decline that befell Spain and the Ottoman Empire in the modern age.

The Ottoman Empire (fourteenth to twentieth century) was still greatly marked by the nomadic origins of the Turks, organising itself as a machine for military conquest. The troops were left with the spoils in return for the victories they fought for. Eventually other forms of payment were added, including ownership of the conquered land with the sole obligation to levy taxes and pass part of them on to the state. Mercenary armies were created to keep the power of the Turkish nobles in check, while the regular army and bureaucracy were accounted for with slaves (youths, originally Christian, seized from their families and trained as faithful servants to the Sultan). In the sixteenth century this model was generalised to the point of absorbing the other occupations taken on by the élite.

[15] See Bairoch (1997, XXII.2.a–b), Weber (1919–20, I.6: 77).
[16] Bairoch (1997: 865).
[17] Bairoch (1997: 864).

Thus the empire's élite came to consist entirely of the Sultan's slaves, who enjoyed power and wealth but could fall from grace at any moment. The Sultan controlled all the sources of wealth, an outcome benefiting from the Sultan's long fight against the notables, but once the notables were defeated the class of personal slaves (the kidnapped youths) abandoned all restraint and eventually prevailed over the Sultan himself. As from the seventeenth century this class appropriated for itself all the land that had been assigned as spoils of war and turned it into latifundia entailing no obligation towards the Sultan. Corruption and nepotism grew rife, to the point of plunging the empire into prolonged decline.[18]

This power structure, resting solely on the wealth gained in war, comprised social communities, often in rivalry, of artisans and merchants ruling the lives of the subjects in accordance with the traditional moral and religious norms. As in the case of China and Spain, Ottoman society never advanced beyond a craft and trade economy. Economic initiative was hamstrung by the religious interdiction of interest. The end of expansion marked the beginning of the decline of the Ottoman Empire, like all the empires based solely on appropriation of the wealth of others. Craft and agricultural activities flourished in other Islamic societies together with a great mercantile tradition, but the social structure and interdiction of interest precluded the development of capitalism.

1.2 Capitalism: Investment and Profit

1.2.1 The Birth of Capitalism. Freedom and Enterprise

Around the year 1000 A.D. Western Europe saw the birth of a new economy thanks to the determination of the most enterprising individuals to shake off the shackles of feudalism. Innovations in agriculture created the conditions for the formation of a surplus, as the economists of the eighteenth century explained.[19] The surplus was invested and this in turn boosted trade and the social division of labour (development of new crafts and professions).

The foundations of capitalism lie precisely in investment, both being used to produce goods and services and sell them. Private investment to

[18] Yapp (1983: 773–782).

[19] E,g. Cantillon (1730, I.15–16), Hume (1752, *Of Commerce*: 293–294), Steuart (1767, I.5), Smith (1776: III.IV, paragraphs 17–18).

increase personal wealth had also existed in the past. In the Jewish tradition it was perfectly legitimate to lend on interest and accumulate wealth through commerce. There is even some evidence of this in the New Testament, in the parable of the servant who keeps the money entrusted to him without putting it a profitable use, for which he is punished by his master. However, such were very limited practices that hardly affected the economy. In Europe the growth of commerce in the Middle Ages boosted production and revived crafts in the ancient Roman cities. Many serfs eluded their feudal obligations and fled to the cities to work as craftsmen.[20] To escape from the feudal lord they placed themselves under the protection of the Bishop—the only authorities left in the cities in the early Middle Ages. For centuries the feudal lords sought to put an end to the flight of the serfs. They had increasingly severe laws introduced by the sovereign to punish the defectors, even with mutilation and death. But it was all in vain.

Many cities were recognised as autonomous (no longer subject to a feudal lord) and obtained privileges to export and import goods. Trade and crafts developed primarily in areas where the political power was weakest and unable to thwart the autonomous powers of the cities. Amalfi flourished, together with various other cities in southern Italy, as well as Venice and, subsequently, the cities of central Italy, while Barcelona, the cities of Provence, Flanders and the Hanseatic League saw similar developments.[21]

In these cities occupations were no longer determined by birth, but gradually became a free choice. The craftsmen organised themselves in corporations, formed citizen armies and fought against the feudal lords, or the sovereign, or indeed the church when they threatened their autonomy. Particularly striking cases were to be seen in the Comunes of northern Italy fighting the emperors—Frederick Barbarossa (twelfth century) and then Frederick II (thirteenth century)—as well as the struggle of the Flemings against the King of Spain (sixteenth century).

On the other hand there was the crusade of the papacy against the Albigensians in the south of France (thirteenth century). However, the corporations set severe limits to free competition, meticulously regulating forms of production and commerce, quantities to produce, and so on. Craft skills were secrets to be conveyed with apprenticeships. Eventually,

[20] See Dopsch (1930, ch. 8: 187–188).
[21] Pirenne (1933, ch. 1).

the corporations became an impediment to development,[22] to the extent that in the eighteenth century Turgot suppressed them in France as an obstacle to free trade.[23]

The fourteenth century saw the first factories for production with hundreds of waged workers in a number of centres including Florence, Bruges and Lyon. Differentiation between entrepreneurs and merchants began to emerge around the sixteenth century. The entrepreneur would purchase the workshop and share the tasks amongst the workers, who thus became specialised. The artisan was now losing ownership of the workshop and control of the production process to become a waged employee, like those who had worked under him. Thus manufacture developed with the first form of capitalistic organisation of production.[24]

The wool industry drove the big landowners to destroy the feudal regime that they themselves had so fiercely defended against the defecting serfs. Above all in Spain and England (the countries producing the finest quality wool), the landowners illegally privatised land with enclosures to be used as pasture land for sheep whose raw wool they sold to the Florentine and Flemish spinning mills. This was the heaviest blow to feudalism in its fight against capitalism.

1.2.2 The Cultural Roots

Why was capitalism born in the West? There is no single cause; there were various factors, but they converged to engender that aspiration for freedom of individuals that is not found in other social systems. In the first place, there is critical, rational research as an activity different from and independent of religious beliefs and moral precepts. The philosophy that was born in Greece in the sixth century BC differs from other systems of thought in that it gave rise to the scientific method that recognises no authority in research and sets store by the individual as a rational being. Mokyr paints a similar picture describing how Europe, unlike Jewish, Chinese and Islamic culture, freed itself from the authority of traditional culture and the institutions in the modern age.[25]

[22] Weber (1919–20, ch. II.3).
[23] Roncaglia (2001: 106).
[24] Marx (1867), *Capital I*, ch. 12.
[25] Mokyr (2017: 2–4).

Christianity introduced other elements, like the idea that all men are equal as children of God. This principle deprives social differences of characterisation as natural differences. Moreover, the conception of sin and individual repentance removes moral behaviour from the domain of custom, making of the individual the centre of moral action, attributed with personal responsibility.

Besides ideas, the organisation of society, too, played a decisive role in the birth of capitalism. In the early Middle Ages in Western Europe the lack of slaves led the monks to take on free peasants to revive agriculture, with the obligation to improve the conditions of the land (the emphyteusis contract). Unlike eastern monasticism, mystical and contemplative as it was, the western monks elevated work to a moral principle. Indeed, the first monastic rule brought in by St Benedict in the sixth century had the motto "*Ora et labora*" (pray and work).

Another major factor lay in the clash between the religious and political powers. Outside Europe either the two fused together or one power prevailed over the other. For example, in the Eastern Roman Empire political power very soon prevailed over religious power, while in the West, with the fall of the Roman Empire, the papacy was induced to pursue hegemony for many centuries. However, the pursuit proved unsuccessful. A conflict arose between the two powers—lasting to the nineteenth century—which eventually led the Europeans to view society not as the product of some superior authority but as the source of various powers.

Antiauthoritarian aspirations were inherited and reprocessed by humanism and the Renaissance. At the end of the Middle Ages individuals acquired independent dignity. Man, said the humanists, is at the centre of the universe and encapsulates it within himself. And among his legitimate aspirations is the will to enrich himself.[26] The aspiration to enrichment is viewed with suspicion in all the static economies. In fact, when the wealth of a social group does not grow, personal enrichment appropriates part of it rather than adding to it. Aristotle condemned enrichment with an aphorism that dominated Western culture for two thousand years: "The enrichment of one is impoverishment for another". Thus the desire for enrichment is destabilising and antisocial. The same idea of a zero-sum economy cropped up repeatedly among all the ancient and mediaeval

[26] See e.g. Manetti (1452: 427–487).

authors including, for example, St Jerome (fourth to fifth century), St Thomas (thirteenth century) and even Montaigne (sixteenth century).[27]

The aphorism against enrichment relates to another famous Aristotelian interdiction, namely of interest on loans, then called usury. This, Aristotle held, is unnatural because money is not a good that satisfies a need but only a means.[28] The rediscovery of Aristotle in the Middle Ages (by the Arabic philosophers) reinforced the diffidence towards monetary interest. However, the scholastic philosophers were up against a great difficulty since they should have condemned the entire new economy which was rapidly growing in Europe. And yet a thirteenth-century Franciscan monk, Peter of John Olivi, contradicting Aristotle, legitimised monetary interest. He explained that money used as capital is different from money used for consumption; it is like seed that proves fruitful and generates more than it contains.[29] Three centuries later the Calvinists renewed criticism of Aristotle's thesis against usury in tougher terms.[30]

The legitimacy of enrichment and dignity of labour, asserted by the humanists and subsequently by the Calvinists, also found application in the case of the merchant's work. This clashed with a thousand-year long negative tradition, bringing in an ethic of commerce.[31] Subsequent to these principles, capitalist culture asserted the general rights of the individual: the right to life, safety and freedom (*habeas corpus*), to the ownership of what one produces, a fair trial, and, finally, freedom of conscience.[32] In the course of the centuries the growth of freedoms and rights was matched by increase in productivity and wealth. This connection gave rise to a historically unique mechanism of economic and civil progress. So much was understood by the major thinkers of the late seventeenth century and the Enlightenment.[33]

It is also in Enlightenment thought that we find the best analysis of free competition. Quesnay demonstrated that the economy grows only if there

[27] Aristotle [1990], *Politics*, 1258b, 1–2; *Nicomachean Ethics*, 1132a–b, Jerome, *Epistulae*, "Ad Edibiam": 980–106, Thomas Aquinas, *Summa theologiae. Secunda secundae*, vol. 41, Quaestio 118.1, reply 2: 243, Montaigne (1580, ch. 22).

[28] Aristotle [1990], *Politics*, 1267a–b.

[29] Olivi [1980], *De usuris*: 111–112.

[30] See e.g. Dumoulin (1546: 113).

[31] See e.g. Peri (1638).

[32] See e.g. Locke (1690), Beccaria (1764), Montesquieu (1748).

[33] E.g. Locke (1690, II.4).

is competition to select the most efficient,[34] while Smith showed that trade is based on reciprocal advantage, underlying the dignity of the individual.[35] It is trade, Smith wrote, that gave rise to the division of labour, which is the source of increase in productivity and technical progress (see Chap. 3).

The fight for freedom and guarantees gradually led to bottom-up control of the institutions. Increase in the surplus was progressively distributed through new social strata. This in turn favoured refinement of customs and the spread of education. The virtuous circle between increase in consumption (i.e. in well-being) and in production enhanced individual responsibility and—among other things—led to the emancipation of women.

Some historians have also included among the cultural factors generating capitalism the idea of progress. Actually, it was capitalism that generated the idea of progress, and not the reverse. Before Bayle, Locke and Mandeville progress had not been theorised.[36] The idea had found circulation only in Athens among the rationalists of the fifth century BC, although they saw it solely in terms of evolution from the past to present times, without contemplating future prospects.[37]

1.2.3 The Fight against Rent

The rent economy was based on privileges acquired de facto or recognised by the law. The elites of this economy appropriated a major part of the social wealth; with no respect for personal merit and great respect for possession of land, they tended towards arbitrary and corrupt practices. There are a number of masterpieces of world literature offering scathing depictions of the class of *rentiers*, from Gogol's "Dead Souls" to Tommasi di Lampedusa's *Il Gattopardo* (The Leopard)—although Veblen (1899) paints a similar picture of the *rentiers* of capitalism.

Be that as it may, capitalism emerged from the fight against feudal rent pursued over the centuries. Western feudalism found legitimation in the universal power of the Empire and the papacy. In practice, however, it took the form of a hierarchy of local big and small bosses enjoying ample

[34] Quesnay (1766: 895–896, 911–912).
[35] Smith (1776, I.II, paragraph 2).
[36] See Locke (1690), Bayle (1704), Mandeville (1705).
[37] See Perrotta (2004: 15–18).

autonomy which often led to arbitrary practices. Thus in practice mediaeval universalism evolved into closed and stifling localism, full of interdictions and taxes on all forms of transaction, transport and business.

To counteract these constraints, the capitalist economy abandoned the universalistic/localistic spirit to acquire a status at the level of the state, although it remained active in international trade amongst the states.[38] The attack led by the new urban productive classes (merchants, artisans, professional figures) on feudal rent would have had no success without the support of the sovereigns. Productive classes and sovereign had a common enemy—the feudal lords, who set up resistance against both the authority of the sovereign and the new urban economy.

The only way to subdue the feudal lords was to deprive them of their prerogatives to administer justice and create a national army. However, it took a lot of money to put together an army, a judiciary and administration that depended directly on the sovereign. This was possible only in the big states and on the strength of loans by the major merchants. Where alliance was achieved between the state and the modern productive classes, capitalistic development went ahead. Such was the case in Holland and England, as well as the Scandinavian countries and, later, France.

In Portugal, Spain and southern Italy, on the other hand the nobles of feudal origin imposed an economy based on agricultural rent, a system of privileges, the right of primogeniture, a parasitic practice resistant to change. These states languished in immobility to the extent of becoming poor despite the fantastic riches that Spain and Portugal drew from their colonies.

Nor, indeed, did modern capitalism succeed in taking off in central-northern Italy and Germany. The major states of Italy's Centre-North, wealthy as they were, were directly dominated by the great mercantile bourgeoisie, but had far too weak national identity and were in eternal strife amongst themselves for hegemony. None were to prevail over the others since as from the seventh century the papacy had obstructed the formation of a united kingdom, which would have jeopardised its independence. Like the papacy in Italy, it was the Empire that held Germany back. The country was fairly rich and developed, but too divided by a multiplicity of small principalities which clung to their autonomy. Above all it was dominated by the Free Imperial Knights, the Emperor's ambiguous feudal lords.

[38] Heckscher (1931, I.1 and I.8).

In France the sovereign—in particular Louis XIV—succeeded in divesting the nobility and the church of their powers at the political level but had no choice but to leave their rents, fiscal privileges and property intact. The new entrepreneurial and professional classes grew amid countless obstacles that failed to set in motion such a development of capitalism as would have overturned power relations. The result was disarray in the public finances, which led to the revolution of 1789.

In general, rent—even when it ceased to be the major source of income—remained a heavy weight on the capitalistic productive process. Even today, in England—together with Holland the cradle of modern-day capitalism—half of the land belongs to 25,000 owners, less than 1% of the population.[39]

1.3 The Data on Progress

Before the modern age, 75–80% of the population were occupied in agriculture and the other primary activities. The birth-rate stood at around 40 per thousand, the mortality rate roughly 38 per thousand.[40] In the mid-sixteenth century the world population was about 500 million, in 1800 a billion, and in 1928 two billion. The population growth rate peaked in 1963, after which growth went at a more moderate rate.[41]

On the evidence of an Infogram graph, at the beginning of the Christian era India's share of the world GDP was 32%, Chinese was 25.4%, one of the group of United Kingdom, France and Germany came only 3.7%. In 1500 China and India together were still at nearly 50%, but the European group had risen to almost 9%. This trend became increasingly pronounced until, in 1870, the European group stood at 22%, China at 17% and India at 12.2%. In 1950 the US took the lead with 27.3%, while the European group came to 15.6% and China and India had very small shares (4.6% and 4.2% respectively). Naturally, the subsequent data show the extraordinarily rapid recovery of China, which stood at only one point below the USA in 2008.[42]

According to Max Roser, up to 1650 Great Britain was locked in the Malthusian trap, to the effect that increase in wealth translated into

[39] Hetherington (2019).
[40] Piuz (1997: 78, 82, 84).
[41] OWD (*Our World in Data*), Population—World population growth.
[42] Infogram, Share of world GDP throughout history.

increase in population rather than per capita income. The data conjectured by Piketty for the whole world up to 1700 reflect the same interpretation.[43] However, the effects of the Malthusian trap should not be exaggerated. Before those dates investments had been growing for centuries. Roser also shows in a graph (ibid.) that in the period 1300–1800 Spain's per capita GDP remained more or less steady at nearly a thousand dollars; Portugal had arrived at $1500 by the mid-sixteenth century, but only for two centuries, with a subsequent drop. Italy had already reached $2000 by the fifteenth century, but then declined; in the seventeenth century Holland came above $2500 while Sweden peaked at $1750 around the year 1700. The Malthusian trap had no effect for any of these countries, and the per capita income seems to have been determined above all by growth or lack of growth in wealth.

Again, it was Roser who calculated that before the modern age life expectancy had stood at around 30 years all over the world, and that it began to grow steadily only in the early years of the nineteenth century. In 1800 stood at 40 years in France and Great Britain (as well, possibly, as Holland), while the other western European countries lagged far behind. And yet a century and a half later—the period of intensive industrialisation—it ranged between 60 and 70 years in Western Europe, the USA and Japan.[44]

In 1705 the average daily per capita intake of calories in France came to 1675 (insufficient, considering that it should average around 2500 in temperate climates). Nevertheless, by 2012 the level had reached about 3500 in all the developed countries.[45] In the course of the sixteenth century the level of literacy in the major countries of Western Europe reached 20%, but it was only at the end of the nineteenth century that the world caught up with this level.[46] Braudel held that it was only in the eighteenth century that the cyclic succession of economic events came to an end and constant increase in wealth set in.[47] But the great historian was underestimating the enormous progress of the previous centuries.

Real progress in the field of health developed only at the end of the nineteenth century, with the discovery of bacteria, compulsory

[43] OWD, Growth & Inequality—Economic Growth, Max Roser ed. Piketty (2014: 73).
[44] OWD, Population—Life expectancy.
[45] FAO data (see OWD, Food—Food per person).
[46] UNESCO and OECD data (see OWD, Education—Literacy).
[47] Braudel (1977: 30–31).

vaccination and the spread of standards of hygiene. In 1872 the infant mortality rate below the age of five still stood at 44% in Italy, as compared with 25% in France and Great Britain. By 1950 the percentages came to: Italy, 8.9%; France, 5.7%; Great Britain, 3.7%. However, in 1955 Brazil was still lagging behind at 19.7%, with India at 25% and China at 26.8%.[48]

Smallpox had been eliminated in central-northern Europe by around the year 1900, and in southern Europe and North America after 1940, while in Brazil and an area stretching from Iran to Indonesia it was only in the 1970s that it finally disappeared.

Malaria was eliminated in Europe in 2000, although it has hung on in Asia, and above all in Africa, where it hit nearly 400,000 people as recently as 2015. Polio (the vaccine for which had been discovered only in 1955) has now been almost completely eradicated. The incidence of tetanus fell by 96% between 1990 and 2016, but there are still 33,000 cases in southern Asia, and as many in Africa (2017).[49]

The female mortality rate associated with pregnancy and childbirth (which, like infant mortality, depends largely on hygiene) began to drop drastically only in the early years of the twentieth century, when in Europe it stood somewhere between 100 and 150 deaths per 100,000 children born.[50]

References

Aristotle [1990] *Politics*, in Id., *Works*, vol. II, Chicago: Encyclopaedia Britannica, 2 vols., reprint, 1990.

Bairoch, Paul (1997) *Storia economica e sociale del mondo* (trans. of *Victoires et déboires. Histoire économique et sociale du monde du XVIe siècle à nos jours*), Torino: Einaudi, 1999.

Bayle, Pierre (1704) *Continuation des pensées diverses*, in Id., *Oeuvres diverses*, vol. 3, reprint, Hildesheim: Olms, 1966.

Beccaria, Cesare (1764) *Dei delitti e delle pene*, Milano: Mursia, 1973.

Bevilacqua, Piero (1996) *Latifondo*, entry of *Enciclopedia delle Scienze sociali*, vol. V, Roma: Istituto dell'Enciclopedia Italiana.

Borsa, Giorgio (1977) *La nascita del mondo moderno in Asia orientale*, Milano: Rizzoli.

[48] OWD, Population-Child mortality.

[49] OWD, Health—respectively, Smallpox, Malaria, Polio, Tetanus.

[50] OWD, Health—Maternal mortality.

Braudel, Fernand (1977) *La dinamica del capitalismo*, trans. from English (*After Thoughts on Material Civilization and Capitalism*, 1977), Bologna: il Mulino.

Brentano, Lujo (1923) *Le origini del capitalismo*, trans. from German, Firenze: Sansoni, 1968.

Breuer, Stefan (1994) *Imperi*, entry of *Enciclopedia delle Scienze sociali*, vol. IV, Roma: Istituto dell'Enciclopedia Italiana.

Cantillon, Richard (1730) *Essai sur la nature du commerce en général*, London: Macmillan, 1931 (also English text).

Cavalli, Alessandro (1974) *Le origini del capitalismo*, Torino: Loescher.

Cutrona, Santina (2012) "Riforme e controriforme", in C. Perrotta and C. Sunna (2012): 91–100.

Dopsch, Alfons (1930) *Economia naturale ed economia monetaria nella storia universale*, trans. from German, Firenze: Sansoni, 1967.

Dumoulin, Charles (1546) *Tractatus contractuum et usurarum*, partly in Arthur Monroe, ed., *Early Economic Thought* (1924) Cambridge, MA: Harvard UP, 1927, trans. into English.

Heckscher, Eli (1931) *Mercantilism*, London and New York: Allen & Unwin and Macmillan, 2nd ed., 1955, trans. from Swedish.

Hetherington, Peter (2019) "So 1% of the People Own Half of England. Inheritance Tax Reform Could Fix That", *The Guardian*, 18 April 2019, online.

Jerome, *Epistulae*, in *Patrologiae Latinae tomus CXX*, J.P. Migne, ed., Turnoholti (Belgium).

Locke, John (1690) *Two Treatises on Government*, in Id., *Works*, reprint, Aalen: Scientia, 1963, vol. 5.

Mandeville, Bernard (1705) *The Grumbling Hive*, in Id., *The Fable of the Bees* (1705–29), Oxford: Clarendon, 1924.

Manetti, Giannozzo (1452) *Della dignità e dell'eccellenza dell'uomo*, IV, in Garin Eugenio, ed., *Prosatori latini del Quattrocento*, Milano and Napoli: Ricciardi, 1952.

Marx, Karl (1867) *Capital I*, trans. from German, Moscow: Progress Publishers, www.marxists.org/archive.

Mokyr, Joel (2017) "The Market for Ideas and the Great Enrichment", paper presented at EHES meeting, Antwerp, May 2017, online.

Montaigne, Michel de (1580) *Essays. Livre 1*, Paris: GF-Flammarion, 1969.

Montesquieu, Charles (1748) *De l'Esprit des lois*, in Id., *Oeuvres complètes*, Paris: Didot, 1838.

Olivi [1980] Peter of John, *De usuris*, in G. Todeschini, ed., *Un trattato di economia politica francescana... di Pietro di Giovanni Olivi*, Roma: Ist. Storico Italiano per il Medioevo, 1980.

OWD (Our World in Data), ed. Max Roser, online: https://ourworldindata.org/

Peri, Giovanni Domenico (1638) *Il negoziante*, Venezia: Hertz, 1697.

Perrotta, Cosimo (2004) *Consumption as an Investment*, London and New York: Routledge.
Perrotta, Cosimo and Sunna, Claudia, eds. (2012), *L'arretratezza del Mezzogiorno. Le idee, l'economia, la storia*, Milano: Bruno Mondadori.
Piketty, Thomas (2014) *Capital in the Twenty-First Century*, Cambridge, MA and London: Harvard UP, trans. from French ed. (2013) and updated.
Pirenne, Henri (1933) *Storia economica e sociale del medioevo*, trans. from French, Milano: Garzanti, 1967.
Piuz, Anne-Marie (1997) *Le economie tradizionali in Europa*, in Bairoch: 77–122.
Quesnay, François (1766) *Sur les travaux des artisans. Second dialogue*, in *F. Quesnay et la Physiocratie*, Paris: INED, 1958, vol. 2: 885–912.
Roncaglia, Alessandro (2001) *The Wealth of Ideas. A History of Economic Thought*, trans. from Italian, Cambridge: CUP, 2006.
Schefold, Bertram (2019) *The Significance of Economic Knowledge for Welfare …*, in Frangipane, Pöttinger, Schefold, eds., *Ancient Economies in Comparative Perspective*, Springer, forthcoming.
Sideri, Sandro (2010) *L'India e gli altri*, ISPI (Istituto di Studi di Politica Internazionale), online.
Smith, Adam (1776) *Wealth of Nations*, E. Cannan, ed. London: Methuen, 1904, online: Library of Economics & Liberty.
Steuart, James (1767) ... *Principles of Political Oeconomy*, vol. 2 Chicago University Press 1966.
Thomas Aquinas *Summa theologiae*, London and New York: Eyre and McGraw Hill, *Secunda secundae* (questions 101–122), vol. 41, 1972, Latin and English text.
Tinker, Hugh R. (1983) *Indian Subcontinent, History of the —*, entry of *The New Encyclopaedia Britannica*, 15th ed., vol. 9: 334–430.
Veblen, Thorstein (1899) *The Theory of the Leisure Class*, online: moglen.law.columbia.edu.
Weber, Max (1919–20) *Storia economica*, trans. from German, Roma: Donzelli, 1997.
Yapp, Malcom E., et al. (1983) *Ottoman Empire and Turkey, History of the —*, entry of *The New Encyclopaedia Britannica*, 15th ed., vol. 13: 771–797.

CHAPTER 2

The Dark Side of Capitalism and Its Myths

Abstract With capitalism the form of solidarity changes, but the weakest are no longer protected. Conflict between capital and labour represents a continuous thread throughout all the various phases of capitalism. The system has created certain self-celebratory myths. The idea that it is the mission of the West to bring civilisation to the world has justified colonial plundering and slaughter, generating racism. The myth of the harmony of interests dates back a long way, culminating with Smith's invisible hand. Another myth has it that the market is capable of self-regulation and can correct its own errors, going so far as to assert that the less the state intervenes, the better the economy works. Historical experience belies all these myths.

Keywords Solidarity • Capital-labour conflict • Interest • Market • State

2.1 Solidarity and Conflict

2.1.1 The End of Solidarity?

In primitive human groups solidarity was a major factor in evolution, supporting survival and growth in an environment full of pitfalls. This may be why solidarity was a social duty in pre-capitalist societies, especially with regard to the weakest and poorest. In mediaeval Europe, at the dawn of

© The Author(s) 2020

C. Perrotta, *Is Capitalism Still Progressive?*,
https://doi.org/10.1007/978-3-030-48169-8_2

the capitalist economy, constant growth in wealth highlighted, by reaction, the value attached to poverty. The monasteries became great centres for assistance.

In the fourteenth and fifteenth centuries, however, as the capitalist economy found consolidation there was a change in civil values—no longer solidarity towards the poor, but industriousness and capacity for enrichment. Indeed, a certain intolerance of charitable practices—viewed as favouring parasitism—grew and waxed strong to the point of contempt.[1] In the sixteenth century the more radical Protestant sects went as far as condemning the poor as not chosen by God and responsible for their own condition. This gave rise to a doctrinal position of hostility towards solidarity with the poor which found its way into today's neoliberalism. Defoe, Malthus and many other authors criticised charitable practices as encouraging the poor to be lazy.[2] Smith held that only animals and beggars expect their meals from the benevolence of the others rather than exchange between equals.[3]

And yet solidarity does not come to an end. On the one hand, it transformed into an impersonal sense of the community. In feudalism the community spirit was universal, but in practice this abstraction translated into solidarity extended only to acquaintances. With capitalism, however, the new dimension of identity lay in the state, and solidarity became impersonal, translating into respect of the laws and for the citizen.

On the other hand, solidarity as help and assistance—which had never ceased, above all in the Catholic countries—revived with new vigour in the eighteenth and nineteenth centuries, inspired by the humanitarian ideals of the Enlightenment and subsequently by the Christian and socialist movements. The latter came into action in response to the appalling living conditions of the workers during the first industrial revolution.

2.1.2 *Conflict between Capital and Labour*

In capitalism the system rests on the relationship between entrepreneur and waged workers—the source of wealth and profit. However, it is also a source of conflict.[4] Smith provided a lucid explanation of the conflict,

[1] See Bracciolini (1428–29: 267). For other authors, see Mollat (1978: 305–310).
[2] Defoe (1704), Malthus (1798).
[3] Smith (1776, I.II, paragraph 2).
[4] See Franzini and Pianta (2016, 2.2: 79–94).

which always tends to go in favour of the stronger side, that is the entrepreneur. The entrepreneurs, Smith pointed out, have little difficulty in uniting amongst themselves whilst the workers—far greater in number but poorer in cultural and material means—face considerable difficulties. Moreover, while the entrepreneurs were free to form associations the workers were denied the possibility. It was therefore right for the state to intervene in favour of the workers in cases of conflict.[5]

Conflict had been developing since the dawn of capitalistic production. The first rebellions against excessive exploitation of workers in the first factories took on the form of religious movements—as was typical of the Middle Ages—with the plea to return to "evangelical" poverty. The first attacks on simony and the luxuries enjoyed by the clergy were already being made as early as the eleventh and twelfth centuries with such figures as the Patarini in Milan and Arnaldo da Brescia.

Soon, however, these pauperist movements were attacking the feudal culture and economy. At the end of the twelfth century and in the thirteenth century Europe was teeming with "heretical" movements that preached poverty and criticised the corruption of the ecclesiastical hierarchy. Some of them became the object of violent persecution by the church, including, for example, the Dulcinians (led by Fra Dolcino) or the movement of the Apostles in northern Italy, the Waldensians, followers of the former merchant Peter Waldo in Lyon and, above all, the long crusade against the Albigensians, or Cathars, in the province of Languedoc, where a sort of refined society hostile to the feudal lords was flourishing. In other cases the Popes and hierarchy succeeded in controlling and regulating the radical movements, as in the case of the Franciscans and Beguines.

The fourteenth century saw the first strife explicitly rage in the name of wages. After the Black death Europe fell into a serious demographic and political crisis in the mid-century. In Florence the lowest workers in the wool factories, the Ciompi, took to rebellion once again in 1378, demanding representation and recognition of their rights. Eventually their revolt came in for fierce repression thanks to an alliance between merchants and artisans.

Following on after the Ciompi there were countless social revolts, almost always ending up in bloody repression. With the Protestant Reform, the wage revolts once again mixed with religious motivations, beginning

[5] Smith (1776, I.VIII, paragraphs 10–14).

with the war of the German peasants, brutally repressed by the Princes who were egged on by Luther.

It took a very long time for the waged workers to organise themselves to defend their interests, held back by their extreme weakness. The first union-like organisation came about only in the 1830s, in England, with the Chartist movement. However, strikes and unions were held to be illegal throughout the nineteenth century. The level of strife grew intense. In the fascist regimes of the twentieth century unions once again came to be considered formally or de facto illegal. They acquired full legitimacy only in the period of the welfare state.

Structural conflict between capital and labour was denied and delegitimised by all the conservative currents. The Christian forces that sided with the labourers, in competition with the socialists, sought to settle the conflict through reconciliation of interests. With the encouragement of Pope Leo XIII, the Catholics revived the idea of the mediaeval corporations as a model of collaboration between capital and labour.[6] In reality, the model was hardly applicable to industrial factories.

Collaboration between the classes was seen as an alternative to the Marxist idea of the class struggle. Nevertheless, the ideology of the corporations was exploited by the fascist regimes to assert an organicist view of society. This was based on permeation between society and state, against the liberal position which rested on their separation. Ultimately, corporativism turned out to be an antiunion, anti-labour force.[7]

A more effective endeavour to mitigate the conflict between capital and labour came in the context of moderate socialism, with the cooperative movement.[8] The members of the cooperatives—producers or consumers—have a say in the business decisions (at least formally), and follow the rule of not distributing dividends but reinvesting the gains of the enterprise. The cooperatives now enjoy tax incentives and occupy quite a strong position in Europe. On the whole, however, their ability to reform the tougher aspects of capitalism has proved limited.

[6] Leo XIII, encyclical *Rerum Novarum* (1891), Toniolo (1908).

[7] See Rossi (1956), Sylos Labini (2014: 51–54).

[8] Degl'Innocenti (1988).

2.2 The False Celebratory Myths

2.2.1 The Civilising Mission

With capitalism the objective connection between economic and civil progress discussed above (see Sect. 1.2.2) is neither linear nor automatic. The exceptions are many and varied (and persist to the present day), making the connection ever uncertain and precarious. Moreover, civil progress is obviously an unintentional result of the accumulation of wealth. The agents of the capitalistic economy are private, take no interest in civil progress and have always got on equally well with civilised, democratic societies and brutally fierce bloody regimes and practices.

In the nineteenth century the idea gained circulation that capitalism had a civilising mission in the world. Marx limited this mission to the creation of an abundance of material goods which would open the way out of indigence for humankind and create the conditions for the superior civilisation.[9] However, the idea of the mission circulating in European public opinion was very different, asserting the need to colonise the other peoples of the earth, who were incapable of self-government. From the very outset, this ideology served to cover up the spirit of exploitation and sheer robbery that motivated the colonialists. Aimé Cesaire argues that the so-called European civilisation has been incapable of solving the two biggest problems it has generated: that of the proletariat and that of the colonies.[10]

Let us take the case of slavery to begin with. It did not end with the end of antiquity, but proceeded alongside and supported the accumulation of profit (see Sects. 3.2.1 and 4.2). With capitalism slavery is even worse than it had been in ancient times. Then it had been part of the economic structure. The slaves were the spoils of war or had lost their freedom for failure to honour debts. This implied no judgement that they were inferior to free men. With capitalism, on the other hand, slavery—since it was inconsistent with the vaunted rights to freedom—has been justified with the alleged inferiority of the men and women reduced to that condition, giving rise to racism.

Sixteenth-century Spain saw long debate over whether the *indios* had a soul, and so whether they were indeed human. The Dominican Bartolomé de las Casas fought in defence of the *indios* for the whole of his life, and

[9] Marx, *Capital III*, VII.XLVIII.13.
[10] Césaire (1955: 7).

his arguments finally won over.[11] Nevertheless, the trade in African slaves was justified with the "inferiority" of the black. Moreover, the abolition of slavery saw racist hatred engendered in the USA; it is still widespread in the southern states, and has led to thousands of murders and wholesale lynching, almost always left unpunished.

In the mid-nineteenth century, while America's slave labour began to show the first signs of crisis, in Europe racism was revived by Gobineau with the theory of the hierarchy of races (the white race obviously being superior to the others). For a century racism reigned in Europe, taking on a pseudoscientific guise (with positivism, social Darwinism and eugenics) and socialist leanings.[12] In Italy, with his studies in physiognomy Lombroso (1876) theorised the racial inferiority and criminal tendencies of the southerners. This perverse cultural trend went a long way, as we know, eventually leading to Nazi racism and the Shoah. Slavery continues in today's capitalism (see Sect. 6.3).

It must be recognised, however, that racism and xenophobia are not only the result of economic advantageousness but also of nationalism and religious fanaticism (which are being revived today, economic crisis in the West driving the impoverished to seek solutions even though false and irrational). For example, as early as 1492—the year of discovery of the New World, chosen by the historians as the beginning of the modern age—with conclusion of the *reconquista* Arabs, Jews and gypsies were expelled from Spain to preserve the Spaniards' *limpieza de sangre* (purity of blood). Those who remained were compelled to convert to Christianity and were nevertheless persecuted for generations.

Capitalism has also been able to get along with the worst aspects of religious fanaticism. Witch-hunts—leading to torture, rigged trials and the stake—became rife precisely when the new economy was developing, in both the Catholic and Protestant countries, and in Europe and America alike. And today they are freely pursued in Africa, Southeast Asia and Amazonia. Various other horrible practices coexist in the ex-colonies with the logic of profit, including infibulation, widespread in central Africa;[13] the caste system in India, and the way of treating the *dalit* (the

[11] See Tosi (2009).

[12] Sunna and Mosca (2016).

[13] In central Africa the proportion of infibulated women ranges from 25% to over 80% (WHO online, from UNICEF 2013 sources).

untouchables);[14] child brides in Africa, Asia and Latin America[15]; and the killing of albino children in Africa (their bodies supposed to confer magic powers). Today some governments, together with and NGOs and humanitarian associations, are committed to putting an end to these practices. It is a valuable commitment, promoting civil development, but as yet the results are limited.

2.2.2 *Harmony of Interests*

Legitimisation of the pursuit of enrichment is a characteristic of capitalism and thus in contrast with the earlier view of the economy as a zero-sum game. With the old approach, individual interest (in getting rich, for example) had to give way to the interest of the community, which wanted stability in its social pattern. Hence there were very few authors who addressed the subject of harmony between individual and collective interests, just as few found it in themselves to praise trade (which is instigated by individual interest) as a peaceful way to social progress.[16] In our modern times, however, the legitimisation of enrichment implies that individual interest must be in harmony with the collective interest. Capitalism emerges as a system advanced by individual interest and able to generate wealth to the advantage of all.

This principle found currency only gradually, at first amongst the humanists. Poggio Bracciolini wrote that our cities are rich and beautiful thanks to the avidity of individuals. Without avidity we would be poor and unhappy.[17] The same idea was later advanced by Davanzati.[18] The Protestants were the first outside intellectual circles to legitimise enrichment. As Max Weber explained, they sought enrichment as a sign of divine preference (grace). The wealth the merchant accumulates does not serve to be enjoyed or shown off, but only to be invested.[19] However, this ethic, which applies only to the select few, does not imply pursuit of well-being

[14] Today the Dalit number over 200 million in India (see *International Dalit Solidarity Network*, online, May 29, 2013).

[15] Today about 650 million women have had experience as child brides (under the age of 18): 12 million a year (*Girls Not Brides*, online periodical, 2019; UNICEF data).

[16] See Perrotta (2004: 39, 66, 240–241).

[17] Bracciolini (1428–29: 267–275).

[18] Davanzati (1581: 35–36).

[19] Max Weber (1904–05, chs. 2 and 5).

for the whole of society, nor does it seek to reconcile the latter with individual enrichment.

It is only through analysis of the passions that these two aspects can be reconciled. In ancient culture the passions were generally held to be negative as contrasting with reason. The humanists changed this approach with re-evaluation of Epicurus, the great outsider of antiquity. Epicurus offered inspiration to the French free thinkers, who asserted that self-interest is not irrational. As Hirschman brilliantly put it, in modern thought economic interest is the intermediary between the passions and reason: it is rational passion.[20]

Drawing the complex theoretical tangle of the seventeenth century to a conclusion, Mandeville (1705) reasserted the initial approach of Bracciolini, comparing two beehives (which were metaphors of society). The poor, virtuous and somewhat inactive beehive will eventually waste away, while the beehive with the selfish and enterprising population flourishes to the advantage of all. Thus private vices (selfish love of wealth and luxury) become benefit for the community.

The authors of the Enlightenment historicised the time-honoured thesis that contrasted riches obtained with violence (war) with wealth gained through peaceful commerce, attributing the former form of enrichment to the premodern economy and the latter to capitalism.[21] To describe the harmony of interests, Smith used another metaphor that has remained famous, namely that of the invisible hand. Individuals know their own interests better than any government and should be left free to pursue them. Each, following their own interests, also brings about advantages for all. It is as if a providential invisible hand settled individual interests in a collective interest.[22] This view, like Mandeville's, sees the harmony of interests as a spontaneous process.

Smith's metaphor proved so successful that it became the pillar of capitalist ideology. Actually—as demonstrated by, among others, Winch and Roncaglia—Smith's thesis was distorted and taken to a hyper-laissez-faire extreme.[23] In the nineteenth century the extreme interpretation of laissez-faire prevailed. Dunoyer (1830), Bastiat (1850)—who was as highly popular as he was superficial—and other authors extolled the harmony that

[20] Hirschman (1977: 37–47).
[21] See Hume (1742), Montesquieu (1748, XXI.20: 373–374), Galiani (1751: 160–161).
[22] Smith (1776: IV.II, paragraph 9).
[23] Winch (1978), Roncaglia (2005).

would derive spontaneously from total freedom of enterprise, arguing that the state should be reduced to a mere "night-watchman" so as not to disturb the natural functioning of the market. The neoclassical authors inherited this approach and denied that there was any structural conflict between individual and collective interests. Today this extreme version has come back in the form of neoliberalism.

Nevertheless, the mercantilists and many authors of the Enlightenment did not embrace the idea of spontaneous harmony of interests. They saw it as natural that conflict should arise between individual and category interests on the one hand, and the collective interest on the other; in such cases the latter should prevail. For example, Petyt's *Britannia Languens* is one sustained invective against private interests, which—if not controlled—destroy trade, encourage larceny, drive the waged workers to devour one another and undermine the public good.[24]

Josiah Tucker was less extreme but his interpretation ran counter to Smith's spontaneous harmony. Conflict between the interests of the individual merchants and the national interest is—he declared—inevitable, and it is up to the government to see that the latter prevails. Self-interest, Tucker wrote in another book, is the great engine of human progress. But it remains restricted in its selfishness, and must therefore be regulated and directed to prevent reciprocal exclusion of various individual interests leading to impoverishment.[25] Subsequent economic theory has neglected these obvious considerations, and the consequences of this neglect have proved disastrous.

2.2.3 The Self-regulating Market

The capitalistic market, like all markets, arose spontaneously, but when it became established it needed rules. To begin with the rules for market behaviour were simply commonsensical good practices that came into use. The first rule was probably not to deceive the person you are trading with. Trade is a contract in which each of the parties commits to giving something the other needs. There will be no repetition if fair play is not observed. The earliest marketing handbooks, in the seventeenth century, placed great emphasis on the fact that a proper merchant must be an honest, reliable person.

[24] Petyt (1680, e.g. pp. 287–289, 457).
[25] Tucker (1750: 316–318, 1755: 56–58).

In the course of time formal rules were added to the moral rules, codified as legal standards respect of which was to be controlled by the institutions. These standards regulate the timing and typologies of the various forms of trade, with close watch kept on price trends to prevent speculation. They are designed to prevent abuse and control competition to prevent it from degenerating with elimination of the minor agents. The stock exchange and financial exchanges exemplify the need for such standards. The aim of the regulations is to ensure that fair play and the general interest prevail, together with safeguarding of the market itself. In fact, without control the tendencies of the market may well run to extremes, competition giving way to arbitrary practices. Thus the prevalence of the most productive enterprise may give way to the predominance of the strongest. As Marx explained, the market tends to concentrate capital and productive activities, stifling competition.[26]

Precisely to prevent oligopolistic concentration, in 1890, with the Sherman Act, the USA embarked on anti-trust legislation prohibiting cartels (secret agreements on prices between competitors). These laws implicitly recognised that the market is not capable of self-correction but generates a type of competition that, if left to itself, tends to self-destruct. Hence the need for the institutions to regulate the market and protect competition from itself.

Paradoxically, it was precisely this period that saw the neoclassical theory of general economic equilibrium come into circulation, subsequently to become dominant. It is based on postulates that ignore the concentration of capital resources. The equilibrium illustrated by Walras (1874) implies that the economic agents are "atomistic", or in other words small enough to be unable to affect market prices, and that bargaining and price-fixing take place in conditions of perfect competition.

Perfect competition, in turn, presupposes other unrealistic conditions: that there be perfect information for all the agents; that there be no information or transaction costs; that enterprises always aim at the maximum profit (and not, for example, satisfactory and reliable long-period profit); that the economic agents' choices be guided solely by prices; that "maximisation of utility" be the only rational form of behaviour, and so forth. These are the assumptions of neoclassical economics, the stream of thought born in the 1870s which still dominates. Neo-classical

[26] Marx, *Capital I*, ch. 25.2; *Capital III*, ch. 15.I.

economists recognise the lack of realism in these postulates, but hold that their market model serves to clarify the logic of the real processes.

Actually, the contrary result has been obtained. The general economic equilibrium model has obscured the real tendencies and processes, driving the majority of economists in the direction of formal analyses ever more remote from reality, while leaving other economists the onerous task of rediscovering truths that are perfectly obvious. To take just a few examples concerning the market, suffice it to recall Marshall's partial equilibrium, Hayek's information costs, the oligopolies of Berle and Means, Schumpeter and Sylos Labini, and Sraffa's market niches. Today all the economics handbooks refer to what are called market failures, but criticisms of Walras's market model have been passed off as special cases (even Keynes's criticism, through the "neoclassical synthesis") that do not disprove the general theory.

And yet all the developed countries now have anti-trust legislation and active policies for the defence of small enterprises against secret agreements between oligopolies to fix prices out of the market. The latter regulation, we must add, is one of the most often flouted. Anti-trust legislation has succeeded only to a small extent in preventing market degeneration. More often it has slowed down the negative trends without stopping them. As we shall see, in this respect the present situation is disastrous. The multinationals dominate not only the global market but also the national markets unchecked. The big business lobbies often prevail over the political powers, driving them to serve their private interests against the public interest which governments should represent.

It is, in fact, precisely the idea that markets should be left as free as possible, given their self-regulating and self-correcting capacity—although historical experience proves the contrary—that lies behind the chronic weakness of anti-trust policies. And it is this idea that, in the 1980s, with Margaret Thatcher in Britain and Ronald Reagan in the USA, gave rise to the ideology of deregulation (advocated by Milton Friedman, the great opponent of Keynesianism). Originally, deregulation came as a reaction to an excess of administrative and union regulations that weighed down the market. Very soon, however, as the very essence of neoliberalism, it served to give free rein to a wild strain of capitalism devoid of restraint, guarantees of correctness and respective rights, and even of the capacity for development over the long period.

2.2.4 *Accumulation "Hindered by the State"*

Associated with the myth of the market without rules but with a self-correcting capacity another myth found circulation, to the effect that the presence of the state compromises capitalistic accumulation of wealth (see also Sect. 2.2.2). This thesis ignores historical experience, which shows that government intervention has very often proved necessary to support accumulation. This has come about in various ways: protecting exports and the trade of the country's citizens abroad, entering into trade agreements with other states and, above all, implementing public investments to encourage development.

In the sixteenth and seventeenth centuries, in the countries where the bourgeois merchant class had an appreciable weight, the governments made considerable investments in roads, ports and merchant fleets, financed the creation of plant, organised assistance for the poor and found work for them, and compelled the nobles to accept restrictions on the export of raw materials. Where the state carried out these complex interventions, capitalism took off; where it failed to do so (due to the opposition of the feudal lords), the economy declined.

England and Spain represented two contrary models in this period. Privatisation of common land (enclosures; see Sect. 1.2.1) was particularly widespread in these two countries, and gave the big landowners the possibility to produce great quantities of the fine quality wool which Flanders and Florence, among others, wanted for their spinning mills. At the same time, however, the enclosures had deprived the peasants of the means of subsistence (land for them to cultivate, the right to make use of the woods, pastureland and common water sources). Driven away from their land, the peasants poured into the cities to beg.[27]

In England the sovereigns allowed enclosures but put increasing limits to the permits to export raw wool. Moreover, Henry VIII ruled that part of the great estates should be reserved for the cultivation of flax and hemp, which—together with wool—were to serve as raw materials for English manufactures.[28] The Tudor sovereigns themselves, above all Elizabeth I, charged the parishes with the task of collecting charity (which gradually turned into obligatory taxes) to finance the workhouses where the able-bodied beggars were gathered and set to work in exchange for bed and

[27] See Perrotta (2004, ch. 6), Piuz (1997: 106).

[28] On Henry VIII's law of 1531–32, see Eden (1797, vol. III, p. CCXLIII).

board.[29] This policy had been theorised shortly before by Thomas Starkey.[30] English capitalism took off thanks to this policy, which saw public prevailing over private interest. It also had advantages for the private entrepreneurs, who found the way open to create new manufactures. Similar policies were implemented in Holland, France and Tuscany.

In Spain, where the state was weak, the picture was in sharp contrast to all this: the big landowners not only retained the freedom to export raw wool but stood in the way of action to organise the poor and extend manufactures.[31] The gold and silver flooding in from the Americas in huge quantities were left in the hands of the nobles and adventurers or used for military expenditure and public display of pomp. In neither case were they invested. The consequent inflation drove the Spaniards to purchase products abroad, where they cost less, eventually ruining production and enriching the neighbouring countries which, by contrast, invested the gold from Spain in manufactures and trade.[32] In conclusion, as a result of the weakness of the state, Spain began its decline, to end up as a backward economy.

However, the pursuit of economic development by a number of states was not limited to the sixteenth and seventeenth centuries, for in the eighteenth century the Marquis of Pombal revived manufactures in Portugal, reorganising the public administration and education. A similar policy was promoted by Campomanes in Spain and implemented by Charles III. These policies slowed down the decline of the Iberian countries.[33]

The stereotype picture of the Industrial Revolution—which began in England in the 1760s—shows it being launched thanks to the liberalisation of the economy and the withdrawal of the state from entrepreneurial activities. But this was not precisely the case. True, the abolition of a cramping series of duties, taxes and prohibitions, as well as reduction of taxes on capital and profit delivered a boost to industry. But industry also benefited from England's trade wars against Holland and France, increased taxes on personal incomes and a sharp rise in government deficit spending.[34]

[29] For Elizabeth's principal poor law (1601), see Eden (1797, III, pp. CLXVII–CLCCIII).
[30] Starkey (1529–30: 34, 60–62, 113–117).
[31] See Viñas y Mey (1970).
[32] See e.g. Mun (1623: 22–24).
[33] See also Moe (2007) on the great innovations from 1750 to 2000.
[34] See Hudson (1997: 488–489, 496).

In Germany the initial basis for industrialisation came with the customs union decided upon by all the German states (Zollverein, in 1834). List, who had theorised this, wrote a treatise on national development led by the state (List 1841) which set Prussia on the road to industrialisation. In the 1870s Bismarck raised the level of public services for the workers, which in turn catalysed industrial development. In the second half of nineteenth century the modernisation and industrialisation of Japan were planned and largely implemented by the state, while in Italy industrialisation was promoted and financed by the Giolitti governments at the beginning of the twentieth century.

One might imagine that state intervention was necessary only at the take-off stages with the launch of industrialisation, but this was not the case. In the meantime, governments were promoting and guiding all the colonial and neo-colonial policies, implemented with public spending. But the state also intervened in many other circumstances. In the 1930s the fascist regimes saved first the banks and then some of the major industries from failure. In Italy the state created an enormous fund to finance private enterprises (IRI: Institute for Industrial Reconstruction); it also set up great insurance and welfare agencies. Meanwhile, in the USA the democratic government of F.D. Roosevelt intervened with large-scale public works to create jobs (the New Deal).

The measures brought in with the New Deal were salutary but too limited, due in part to the fierce opposition of the conservatives. State intervention—both in the USA and in the right-wing regimes—led commentators to speak of a mixed economy (private and public), but it was Keynes (1936) alone who revolutionised economic analysis. Against the neoclassicals, who imputed the crisis to downward wage rigidity brought about by the unions, Keynes demonstrated that on the contrary the crisis was due to insufficient demand, which afforded the enterprises scant sales prospects, explaining that demand was insufficient precisely because wages were too low.[35]

The result was a vicious circle: excessively low wages failed to generate sufficient demand, which meant scant prospects for sales, and so investment went down and unemployment went up; the increase in unemployment prevented wages from rising, and so on.[36] Keynes realised that *the market was not able to escape from this negative spiral by itself.* To respond

[35] Keynes (1936, chs. 2 and 3).
[36] Keynes (1936, chs. 5–7, 12, 18).

to this underconsumption the state had to intervene, creating job opportunities, boosting employment, and thereby defending the level of wages. This would open the way to reviving investments and refuelling profits. Keynes's proposal—which was in accord with Roosevelt's New Deal—had no time to be tried out before the outbreak of war.

Not long after, Polanyi (1944) demonstrated that the capitalistic market, far from being entirely spontaneous, is organised by the state. After the war, the state once again played the role of protagonist in western development with the creation of the welfare state. And the crisis that put an end to that great adventure, in the 1980s, was due to public guidance foregoing its role in development (see Chap. 5). We are still suffering from this absence, so keenly sought after and theorised by the exponents of neoliberalism.

Fortunately, a new awareness of the indispensable role of the state is now emerging in economic studies. Mariana Mazzucato (2013) has illustrated in detail just how much innovation and entrepreneurship itself—which drives accumulation and prevents stagnation—very often owe to the state.[37] Looking back over the past, Sekera (2018) has tracked down a number of long neglected authors who analysed the central importance of the public economic system.

References

Bastiat, Fredéric (1850) *Harmonies économiques*, vol. VI of Id., *Oeuvres complètes.* Online: bastiat.org, F.R. Rideau ed.

Bracciolini, Poggio (1428–29) *L'avarizia*, in E. Garin, ed., *Prosatori latini del Quattrocento*, Milano-Napoli: Ricciardi, 1952: 248–301, trans. from Latin.

Césaire, Aimé (1955) *Discours sur le colonialisme*, Paris: Présence Africaine, 2004.

Davanzati, Bernardo (1581) *Notizia de' cambi*, in *Notizie mercantili delle monete e de' cambi*, L. Carrero, ed., Venezia: Gondoliere, 1840.

Defoe, Daniel (1704) *Giving Alms no Charity*, in John R. McCulloch, ed., *A Select Collection of Scarce and Valuable Economical Tracts*, London (Lord Overstone) 1859: 27–59.

Degl'Innocenti, Maurizio, ed. (1988) *Il movimento cooperativo nella storia d'Europa*, Milano: F. Angeli.

Dunoyer, Charles (1830) *Nouveau traité d'économie sociale*, then vol. 2 of Id., *De la liberté du travail*, 2 vols., Paris: Guillaumin, 1845.

[37] See also Mazzucato (2018).

Eden, Sir Frederic (1797) *The State of the Poor. A History of the Labour Classes in England …*, 3 vols., London: J. Davies.
Franzini, Maurizio and Pianta, Mario (2016) *Disuguaglianze*, Roma-Bari: Laterza, ebook.
Galiani, Ferdinando (1751) *Della moneta*, in P. Custodi (1803–16), ed., *Scrittori classici italiani di economia politica*, reprint, Roma: Bizzarri, 1965–69, Parte Moderna, vols. 3 & 4.
Hirschman, Albert (1977) *Le passioni e gli interessi*, trans. from English, Milano: Feltrinelli, 1979.
Hudson, Pat (1997) *Rivoluzione industriale*, entry of *Enciclopedia delle scienze sociali*, Roma: Istituto d. Enciclopedia Italiana, vol. VII: 487–501.
Hume, David (1742) *Of the Middle Station of Life*, in Id., *Essays Moral, Political and Literary*, vols. 3 & 4 of his *Philosophical Works* [1882–86] reprint Aalen: Scientia, 1964.
Keynes, John Maynard (1936) *The General Theory of Employment, Interest and Money*, London: Macmillan, 1973.
List, Friedrich (1841) *The National System of Political Economy*, trans. from German, London: Longmans, Green, 1909, online The Library of Economics and Liberty.
Lombroso, Cesare (1876) *L'uomo delinquente*, 5th ed., 1897, Milano: Bompiani, 2013.
Malthus, Thomas Robert (1798) *An Essay on the Principle of Population*, London: J. Johnson.
Mandeville, Bernard (1705) *The Grumbling Hive*, in Id., *The Fable of the Bees* (1705–29), Oxford: Clarendon, 1924.
Marx, Karl, *Capital I* (1867), trans. from German, Moscow: Progress Publishers, www.marxists.org/archive.
———, *Capital III* (1863–83), trans. from German, first ed. 1894, New York: International Publishers, online: marxists.org, 1999.
Mazzucato, Mariana (2013) *Lo Stato innovatore (The Entrepreneurial State)*, Roma and Bari: Laterza.
——— (2018) *The Value of Everything*, Allen Lane and Penguin.
Moe, Espen (2007) *Governance, Growth and Global Leadership*, London and New York: Routledge, 2016.
Mollat, Michel (1978) *Les pauvres au Moyen Age*, Paris: Hachette.
Montesquieu, Charles (1748) *De l'Esprit des lois*, in Id., *Oeuvres complètes*, Paris: Didot, 1838.
Mun, Thomas (1623) *England's Treasure by Forraign Trade …*, 1st ed., 1664., reprint, Fairfield, NJ: Kelley.
Perrotta, Cosimo (2004) *Consumption as an Investment*, London and New York: Routledge.

Petyt, William (1680) *Britannia Languens or A Discourse of Trade*, in John R. McCulloch, *A Select Collection of Early English Tracts on Commerce*, London: Political Economy Club, 1856: 275–504.

Piuz, Anne-Marie (1997) *Le economie tradizionali in Europa*, in Bairoch: 77–122.

Polanyi, Karl (1944) *The Great Transformation*, Boston: Beacon, 2001, online.

Roncaglia, Alessandro (2005) *Il mito della mano invisibile*, Roma and Bari: Laterza.

Rossi, Ernesto (1956) *Aria fritta*, Bari: Laterza.

Sekera, June (2018) "The Public Economy: Understanding Government as a Producer", *Real-World Economics Review*, No. 84: 36–99.

Smith, Adam (1776) *Wealth of Nations*, E. Cannan, ed., London: Methuen, 1904, online: Library of Economics & Liberty.

Starkey, Thomas (1529–30) *A Dialogue between Pole and Lupset*, London: Royal Historical Society—University College, 1989.

Sunna, Claudia and Mosca, Manuela (2016) "Heterogenesis of Ends: Herbert Spencer and the Italian economists", *The European Journal of the History of Economic Thought*, March 2016.

Sylos Labini, Paolo (2014) "La politica economica del fascismo. La crisi del '29", *Moneta e Credito*: 47–54.

Toniolo, Giuseppe (1908) *Trattato di economia sociale*, online: Storiologia.

Tosi, Giuseppe (2009) "Bartolomé de Las Casas ...", *Jura Gentium*, online.

Tucker, Josiah (1750 ca.) ... *On the Advantages and Disadvantages*... [of] *France and Great Britain with Regard to Trade*..., in John R. McCulloch, ed., *A Select Collection of Scarce and Valuable Tracts on Commerce*, London (Lord Overstone), 1859: 309–425.

——— (1755) *Elements of Commerce and Theory of Taxes*, in Id., *A Selection from His Economic and Political Writings*, New York: Columbia University Press, 1931.

Viñas y Mey, Carmelo (1970) "Notas sobre primeras materias, capitalismo industrial y inflación en Castilla durante el siglo XVI", *Anuario de Historia Económica y Social*, Univ. de Madrid.

Walras, Léon (1874) *Éléments d'économie politique pure*, Lausanne: Corbaz, online: Internet Archive.

Weber, Max (1904–05) *The Protestant Ethic and the Spirit of Capitalism*, trans. from German, London and New York: Routledge, 1992.

WHO (World Health Organization) online.

Winch, Donald (1978) *Adam Smith's Politics*, Cambridge: CUP.

CHAPTER 3

Capitalistic Accumulation

Abstract Capitalistic accumulation lies in the constant reinvestment of profit. It continues to fuel the supply of goods as long as demand grows in proportion. Competition amongst the producers of goods drives them to boost productivity through innovation and increasing mechanisation. History shows three ways to accomplish accumulation. One, technologically backward, is based on low wages and produces poverty. Another (the most common) is mechanised, keeps wages low and is exposed to underconsumption. The third, which emerged only in the eighteenth century and with the welfare state, bases increase in productivity on high wages, and thus avoids saturation. Increasing wealth gives rise to the productive middle classes, which carry civilisation forward.

Keywords Competition • Technical progress • High/low wages • Middle classes • Underconsumption

3.1 The Market and Technical Progress

3.1.1 Reinvestment

In pre-capitalist systems the habit of hoarding removed wealth from circulation to conserve it in a sterile state. Capitalistic accumulation, on the other hand, uses the profit generated by investment to make new investments. Thus the wealth grows with each economic cycle.

© The Author(s) 2020

C. Perrotta, *Is Capitalism Still Progressive?*,
https://doi.org/10.1007/978-3-030-48169-8_3

For each cycle the entrepreneurs produce new goods and sell them on the market, which is the place where the supply matches the demand. In the capitalistic market the supply provided by enterprises and the final demand of the consumers tend to grow continually. Everything else follows on from this, both the progressive aspects and the difficulties of accumulation. On the one hand we have increase in wealth, new inventions and industriousness; on the other hand, there is the hazard of stagnation, crisis and unemployment.

3.1.2 Competition and Innovation

In the course of history there have been various types of market (see Polanyi et al. 1957). In the pre-capitalist markets production is generally stable, and so consumption is, too, and supply and demand are easily matched. By contrast, in the capitalistic market, where production runs on a rising trend, competition is generated between entrepreneurs-sellers to win over new consumers. In the Middle Ages, the capitalistic market was limited, being based mainly on the demand of the most well-off households, buying luxury goods. Thus the sellers had to reach out to increasingly distant purchasers. Hence the international fairs, like those of Piacenza, Medina del Campo and Lyon, on which the major European merchants converged in a certain period of the year.

Soon the competition intensified and the producers were driven to seek new profits, not only looking to new, distant markets, but also increasing the profitability of investment (i.e. the ratio between profit and investment). There were two ways to do this: keeping the cost of labour, and thus the wages, low, or boosting the productivity of labour. These two ways are almost always present together, combining to various degrees. However, the prevalence of one or the other of the ways brings about different types of capitalistic accumulation.

With accumulation in which low labour cost is prevalent not only are wages usually low but the workers are poorly skilled and innovations few. An extreme example of this is the slave production or semi-slave production that took place in the Americas in the modern age and which is still being engaged in with the multinationals (see below).

On the other hand, with accumulation that sees increased labour productivity prevailing there should be relatively high wages and a great many innovations. However, there have been few cases of this: in the eighteenth century in North-West Europe and, after the Second World War (with the welfare state) to some extent throughout Western Europe.

But the most common type of accumulation is intermediate, based on intensive mechanisation but low wages. Such was the case in the mercantilist economy of the seventeenth century in Europe (see Furniss 1920) and in the long process of industrialisation spanning from the late eighteenth century to the Second World War.

Innovation—which is the driver of accumulation—is usually brought in by an entrepreneur (individual or collective) to step up competitiveness. Thus a greater profit is obtained, but only for a limited time. When the competitors are compelled to imitate the innovation so as not to lose customers, the levels of competition return to the previous levels and the innovator's extra profit disappears. Nevertheless, the final result is that the general level of productivity is increased and prices are reduced. One example of great innovation was the opening of a new way to reach the Asian markets by circumnavigating Africa, as the Portuguese did in the fifteenth century.

There are various types of innovation that can boost productivity. For example, the productive process can be enhanced when a new machine is brought in, mechanising part of the work and speeding up production. In this case the production costs are reduced and the innovator can offer a lower price. One great innovation came with invention of the steam-boiler, launching the first industrial revolution. An innovation may also change the product, as in the case of the merchants of Lyon, who invented new patterns and colours for their wool fabrics in the sixteenth century. Or, again, it can open up new markets, as in the case of the railways in the mid-nineteenth century.

Thus innovation can affect many aspects of the productive process: a better quality product, faster transport, a new fashion, a new production technique, raw materials that are more durable or cost less, and so forth. The invention of the automobile sustained development throughout the twentieth century. The personal computer, then the cell phone, and then the smartphone have marked the principal stages in the digital and information technology revolution that is still underway.

It must, however, be stressed that it is not only a matter of the great historic innovations. Schumpeter (1911) wrote of swarms of innovations which thicken in certain periods. What, for the sake of brevity, we call technical progress lies in fact in a cluster of myriad innovations of various types promoted through competition and generating a constant growth in wealth.

3.1.3 Market Expansion

The mechanism of competition implies unflagging pursuit of ever new productive processes and products, but also the—no less unflagging—pursuit of increasing demand for goods. This accounts for, among other things, fashion, which attracts consumers not because it satisfies a need, even at the cultural or aesthetic level, but because it represents a novelty. Fashion has always existed, above all in the field of luxury goods, but with capitalism it has become a very effective means to extend the market. In reality, the creators of fashion and its constant changes are in fact the entrepreneurs.

In the sixteenth and seventeenth centuries, there were two factors behind the great expansion due to mercantilist policies: growth of the internal market and conquest of new foreign markets. The internal market grew thanks above all to the increased consumption of the new middle classes: professional figures, the bureaucracy, the army and the high clergy and, above all, the protagonists of development (merchants, entrepreneurs, skilled artisans, money dealers and shareholders).

Wallerstein argues that the expansion outside the "areas external to historical capitalism" was not due to pursuit of new markets because, he holds, demand for the products of capitalism was lacking, and he attributes the expansion to pursuit of cheap labour power.[1] Actually, up to the end of the seventeenth century expansion was mainly accounted for by luxury goods, for which there has always been demand. However, the colonial expansion which Wallerstein seems to have in mind was accomplished above all to appropriate natural resources, including tropical agricultural produce (see Chap. 4). Expansion due to the pursuit of cheap labour power characterised the second half of the twentieth century, and is now catalysed by globalisation.

In the course of the modern age the nobles found themselves losing their old functions of command, and to preserve their prestige they dedicated themselves to ostentation of a luxurious lifestyle. However, in their competition with the rich bourgeoisie they were losers from the outset because their rents—handsome as they may have been—were more or less

[1] Wallerstein (1995: 35).

fixed, while the incomes from profits went on growing (see Sombart 1912). Many nobles brought ruin on themselves in this mad pursuit, and their property passed over to the bourgeoisie.

At the time, as indeed subsequently, it was often wars that decided the fate of trade. England went to war against Holland on various occasions to curb their keen competition in sea transport and fishing, and took military action to compel Portugal to accept terms of trade favourable to the British. Most decisive of all, however, were the colonial wars—the wars of Elizabeth I's pirates against the Spanish colonies in America, or the wars between Dutch, French, British, Portuguese, and so on for dominion in North America, Asia and Africa.

On the internal market, the great turning point came at the end of the seventeenth century. The market for luxury goods showed some difficulty in expanding any further. Then the entrepreneurs and economists discovered the potential of internal expansion, but this meant raising the wages of the skilled workers. Thus there came a dramatic departure from the policies of the seventeenth century. Any decline in profit due to high wages, the British economists argued, was only apparent, for they make the workers more motivated and collaborative, increasing their productivity because they improve the quality of work.[2] This new approach lasted only to the dawn of the Industrial Revolution, but it sufficed to fuel the great culture of the Enlightenment. It was, however, followed by return to the system of high productivity with low wages.

3.2 Three Forms of Accumulation

3.2.1 Resource Grabbing and Slave Labour

Capitalistic accumulation based on slave or semi-slave labour is far more widespread than one might think, both in the modern age and in the present day. It is the most backward and the least civil form of accumulation (see also Chap. 4 and Sect. 6.3).

In general slave labour implies an outdated technology that is not readily updated; the workers' education and qualifications are deliberately kept low; the quality of the product does not improve and investment tends to turn into parasitic rent which goes to small and often very wealthy minorities. This was the practice (and still is) in the mining activities of Africa and

[2] See Janssen (1713).

Latin America, and in the great plantations in the same areas as well as Southeast Asia.

But slave labour is by no means confined to these activities. Today people driven to very hard and badly paid work with no chance of leaving it are effectively slaves, even though not formally the property of a master. Some examples are the immigrants in the oil producing Arab countries, or the emigrants held prisoner in Libya, to be tortured and sold on the market.

Semi-slavery is a condition experienced by many illegal immigrants in the West, working on farms or in covert factories. They are hostages of the gang masters who keep hold of their documents, reduce the pay to the minimum and compel them to live in appalling conditions. Semi-slaves, too, are the millions of women and children in Africa and Southeast Asia who work on clothing for the Western multinationals, or, in atrocious conditions, grow (or fish for) products to be sold in the rich countries, or again mine rare minerals with their hands, exposed to radiation.

Evidently the living conditions of today's slaves are worse than the conditions on the American plantations in the modern age, because today slave labour is performed in a context of keen competition and the master aims to obtain the maximum profit possible from the worker.

3.2.2 Increasing Productivity with Mechanisation and Low Wages

This form of accumulation can yield very high profits, but at the expense of the living and working conditions of the waged workers. As Sweezy writes with reference to Brazil, the capitalists view the masses not as consumers but as cost: the lower the cost, the higher the profits.[3] There have been two major episodes that have seen this type of accumulation dominant: the transition from agricultural to manufacturing economy (in sixteenth and seventeenth century in Western Europe) and the process of industrialisation (eighteenth and nineteenth century).

Transition to a manufacture-dominated economy was a necessary step for capitalism to gain ground. In the agricultural economy production of manufactures is marginal, being subsidiary to agricultural work, while with capitalism it becomes independent of agriculture and sees progressive expansion. In the workshop the organisation of labour becomes increasingly articulated (increasing technical division of labour), until workshop

[3] Sweezy (1981: 79).

evolves into factory. In the latter the production process is rationalised, the tasks divided amongst various groups of workers, and performance speeded up. Expansion of trade is the necessary complement to the expansion of manufacturing.

This process has been repeated along much the same lines in all of the numerous cases of generation and development of the capitalistic economy. Adam Smith described increasing division of labour as the driving force behind increased productivity and economic development.[4] However, Ferguson and even Smith himself, looking to the beginnings of the first industrial revolution, realised that mechanisation impoverishes the workers' intellectual faculties.[5]

In fact, increased productivity was essentially based on mechanisation. The work of the great majority of workers became ever more elementary, laborious and degrading. Children were turned into little slaves, as Bairoch put it.[6] This model of accumulation was applied to all the successive stages of the industrial economy: Taylorism, Fordism and the assembly line.

This trend led to an unsustainable increase in the pace of work, which was described by Marx[7] (and later illustrated by great film directors like Fritz Lang in "Metropolis" in 1927, and Chaplin in "Modern Times", in 1936). In the years 1950–1960 the faster pace obtained with simplification of actions reached the physical limits of resistance of the human body.[8] It was only then that the entrepreneurs and economists began to consider skilled labour as a new way to achieve greater productivity.

In the roughly five centuries that saw the expansion of manufacturing and then industrial production (from the sixteenth to the twentieth century) permanent improvements in wages and working conditions were obtained very late, after the mid-nineteenth century, at the cost of keenly fought union battles and even bloodshed. It was only with the welfare state (about 1950–1980) that the age of low wages ended. Since then, however, the bargaining power of the wage earners has reverted to a downward path, and accumulation based on low wages has been growing again, even in the rich countries (see Chap. 6).

[4] Smith (1776, I.1).

[5] Ferguson (1767, IV.1; V.3: 247–248), Smith (1776, I.1.6; IV.9. 35).

[6] Bairoch (1997: 351–358).

[7] Marx (*Capital I*, ch. 15).

[8] On the effects of automation on the workers, see Tanenbaum (1983a: 513 and 1983b: 599).

3.2.3 *Increased Productivity with High Wages and Growth of Human Capital*

In the third model of accumulation increased productivity is based on high wages; work involves higher skills thanks to education and better living conditions, and technical progress flourishes. As we have seen, there have been only two periods when accumulation based on high wages was dominant: in the eighteenth century, and in the times of the welfare state.

In 1728 Daniel Defoe explained that England, which had the highest wages in the world, could not compete with China and India by saving on the cost of labour. In those countries wages were extremely low and work was carried out in disastrous conditions. The English could compete only on the strength of the better quality of their products, and it was precisely wages that ensured this.[9] In the areas of major development, like the North of England, wages remained high until the 1770s,[10] but started on a steady decline with the beginning of the Industrial Revolution.[11]

Some authors of the Enlightenment described qualification for work as investment by the individual in study or specialisation that would guarantee higher future earnings.[12] And Smith added that by extension individual qualification transmutes into qualification of society. A sort of social capital, he wrote, is achieved and enhances the general productivity of the system.[13]

This was a brilliant insight, and it found confirmation in the second half of the nineteenth century. In that period enterprises found themselves short of technicians able to manage an economy growing increasingly complex, not only for intervention on and running of machinery but also for administrative and marketing techniques. The response to the pressure exerted by enterprises came not only with obligatory primary education,[14] but also vocational schools, technical institutes and engineering and science faculties in general.

The increased productivity due to skilled labour became the new factor of accumulation. After a long series of studies and theories, in the 1960s some Chicago economists including, in the first place, Theodore Schultz

[9] Defoe (1728, I.1: 36–45, 59–68).
[10] Gilboy (1936).
[11] Bairoch (1997, ch. VIII).
[12] See e.g. Cantillon (1730, I.7–8), Smith (1776, I.10.9–10).
[13] Smith (1776, II.1.17).
[14] See the World Bank data processed by OWD, Education—Primary and Secondary.

(1961), theorised investment in human capital. However, Schultz focused his analysis on education; the great sectors of research, comfort and widespread culture as means for qualification of human capital remained in the shade.

3.3 The Growth of the Middle Classes

3.3.1 *The Middle Classes that Contribute to Accumulation*

The tenth and eleventh centuries saw an increase in the productivity of agriculture which generated a stable surplus (see Sect. 1.2.1). An intermediate space then opened between the elites in possession of the rents and the direct producers of wealth, namely the workers of the agricultural economy. In this space new crafts and occupations arose, responding to the new needs of the urban economy. They created the possibility for a more articulated social organisation and more efficient production. This led in turn to the growing social division of labour that opened the way to modern society.

To begin with, the middle classes consisted of artisans and merchants/entrepreneurs, including the gentry (the country squires who promoted capitalism in England). Soon, however, they were joined by various professional figures: doctors, notaries, architects, jurists, money dealers and bankers. Gradually the category of civil servants and public employees expanded, with judges, researchers and teachers, the military top brass, and so forth. Later on still came a proliferation of intellectuals and artists and, finally, technicians to tackle the growing complexity of the machinery. The latter grew in number with the increasing specialisation and division of labour in manufacturing activities.

All these classes were seen to constitute the bourgeoisie, in contrast with the aristocracy of the land and warlords. The individuals in these classes came into competition with one another in their crafts or professions. They did not seek privileges, but claimed rights and recognition of merit. To these classes European civilisation based on the impersonal nature of laws and regulations owes its origins. It is they that promoted the liberal revolutions against the aristocracy, in England in the seventeenth century, in America and France in the eighteenth century, and in the whole of Europe in the nineteenth century. And yet once they became the dominant class, the bourgeoisie in turn generated a new élite; the élite of the wealthy, often enjoying rents which, as Veblen (1899) brilliantly explained, also burgeoned in the capitalist economy.

The rest of the middle class (the majority), having no rent to live on, depended on their own work. They did not always maintain the progressive, liberal spirit of the early days, keen to distinguish themselves from the lower classes in terms of income, culture and social status. The closer they were to the lower classes, the more insistent was their opposition to them. With the threat of losing that status, in the early twentieth century many members of the middle class were driven to authoritarian and antidemocratic solutions. A similar process is developing in the rich countries today in reaction to the economic crisis hitting the lower middle classes in particular.

The prevalence of the middle classes differentiates Western Europe from China and India. In the seventeenth and eighteenth centuries these two great countries—but also Thailand, Vietnam and Indonesia—had economies that were on the whole as rich and highly developed as those of Western Europe. And they were technically well-equipped—China decidedly more so than Europe (see Sects. 1.1.3 and 4.4).[15] So why did these countries fail to take the lead, actually becoming impoverished as Europe advanced? According to the majority of historians it was due to the Industrial Revolution, representing a great advantage for Europe.

Actually, for example, the industrial revolution offered British colonialism the means to destroy India's textile industry, which had been in competition, and to lay waste the Chinese economy with the Opium Wars (see Sect. 4.4). But again, why was there no trace of an industrial revolution in China or India despite the large-scale manufacturing production? The reason lies in the lack of interest in profit, and the social structure that had formed around it (see Sects. 1.1.2 and 1.1.3).

In Europe the profit economy had been prevalent for centuries, although ample areas of symbiosis or accommodation with the rent system remained. For centuries capitalistic accumulation had seen the extension of manufacturing, absorbing labour force from the rural areas. Famine and poverty, illiteracy and superstition, on which the dominion of agrarian rent has rested in every country, slowly diminished in the West. At the same time, however, there was a growing awareness of rights, which later also spread to the factory workers, spurring them to fight for better living and working conditions.

[15] Bairoch (1997, XVII.I.d–e).

3.3.2 *The Middle Class Dependent on Rent*

Naturally, some middle classes also existed in the economies dominated by rent, but they were marginal. The elites of these economies consisted of big landowners, and in some cases also merchants of some standing (as in the Arab countries, Armenia, Greece and the Jewish communities among others). In China, midway between the elites and merchants, there was the Chinese gentry—the Mandarins or shenshi (see Sect. 1.1.3), depending partly on the state and partly on what they could obtain with agrarian rent.

In general, however, the middle classes depend, directly or indirectly, on rent in the non-capitalist economies. They emerge in response to the need to provide private or public services to the ruling class. Middle classes enjoying rents are still particularly numerous in Mediterranean and Eastern Europe, including Russia, as well as the Latin American colonies that have inherited the social structure of Spain and Portugal and the former colonies on all the continents. In all these economies the per capita wealth is low, concentrated in a few hands, mainly of the farmers, shipowners (as in Greece) and big merchants. The result is immense private wealth and glaring social inequality.

In these cases the middle class shares some of the privileges of the elites. In general it lacks innovative flair, distrusts every form of democracy, despises labour, solidarity and civic sense, and harasses manual workers. The model it pursues is the parasitic, leisurely life of the landowner.[16] This class plays a decisive role in the formation of the conservative social block that rules rent economies.

Very often, in the Latin American countries, Southeast Asia, the Middle East, and now some African countries, the middle class has merged with the old elites, forming a military-agricultural or military-financial complex that holds authoritarian sway over the country, albeit at times under the guise of formal democracy.

3.4 Unemployment, Saturation, Underconsumption

Technical progress—either in the form of mechanisation or in other forms—is the fundamental agent of capitalistic accumulation, being the main source of increase in productivity. However, while on the one hand

[16] For the public sector, see Bold et al. (2017).

it lowers the cost of individual goods, on the other hand it leads to ever greater overall production and thus tends to saturate the market. At the same time, it replaces labour with machines, creating new areas of unemployment.

The unemployment thus generated—called technological unemployment—reduces the purchasing power of the workers as a whole and so lowers market demand. This comes about in two ways. On the one hand, with fewer employed there are fewer paying consumers, while on the other hand the unemployed, being prepared to accept lower wages, bring downward pressure to bear on the wages of the employed. So it was that Marx called this type of unemployment the "reserve army of labour".[17]

For example, the introduction of mechanised looms was already creating unemployment in the sixteenth century and, as we have seen, the luxury goods market was already approaching saturation by the end of the seventeenth century. At the beginning of the Industrial Revolution, the mechanical loom—introduced in 1769—provoked a rebellion under the leadership of Ned Ludd (a historically uncertain figure).

In the second decade of the nineteenth century the Luddites (followers of Ludd) set about destroying the new machines, causing further unemployment.[18] Ricardo observed that they were misguided, because the increase in productivity afforded by the new machines would generate higher profits and thus greater investment leading to greater employment.[19] However, his friend Barton pointed out to him that new investments could boost employment only if they were used to take on new workers. If, on the other hand, they went into more machines—a highly likely outcome—employment would not increase but fall yet further.[20] Subsequent to Barton's observations, Ricardo admitted that in reality over the long period the increase in employment would not offset the harm brought to the dismissed workers by technical progress (Ricardo, ibid.).

But Ricardo did not take his self-criticism to the ultimate conclusions. Barton's objection was indeed relevant, because technical progress normally favours new investments in machinery and not in workers. This means that accumulation creates an imbalance between supply (in excess) and demand (insufficient) which tends to get worse. The first to decry this

[17] Marx, *Capital I*, ch. 25.3.
[18] Bairoch (1997: 622–623).
[19] Ricardo (1821, ch. 31).
[20] Barton (1817: 40–45).

tendency were the theoreticians of underconsumption, as they came to be known, and in particular Malthus and Sismondi. In the early years of the nineteenth century they observed that there were recurrent crises that left part of the production unsold, attributing this to excessive production.

The solution Malthus proposed was to reduce investment and instead increase unproductive consumption (that of the landowners and the civil servants).[21] Sismondi attributed the crises to excessively low wages which translated into insufficient demand and proposed both raising wages and restraining technical progress.[22] According to the other classical economists, however, these solutions were contrary to the logic of capitalistic accumulation: to begin with, there was no sense in spending the surplus unproductively; then, the level of wages should be left to be determined by competition; and, finally, there could be no halting technical progress.[23]

In practice, not knowing how to account for the periodical crises, the classical economists denied them. First, they did so with J.B. Say's law, which states that capitalistic investment consists of making purchases of labour (paid with wages) and of the means of production. These acquisitions create in advance on the market the necessary resources to bring about an increase in demand, which will absorb the entire final product of the investments themselves.[24]

Another argument against the underconsumption theories lay in the business cycle. J.S. Mill interpreted the periodical crises as short-period fluctuations which are due to temporary imbalances between demand and supply in the market. Such fluctuations are, in fact, cyclical and inevitable, but are equally inevitably surmounted by the market (Say had called them disproportion crises).[25] Actually, Mill confused the fluctuations of the business cycle with structural crises which are not due to temporary imbalances, and which the market is unable to surmount.

In reality Say's law is a matter of begging the question, since it takes as given what needs to be demonstrated. And yet it is still accepted in orthodox economics. Even worse is the story of the business cycle theory, which was even accepted by Marx, and still rules uncontested. The very concept

[21] Malthus (1820: 401–405).

[22] Sismondi (1819: 312–368, 443–448).

[23] Ricardo (1820: 198, 245), Torrens (1819).

[24] Say (1803, II, 15). For an extreme version of Say's law, see Mill, J. (1808: 81–88) and Mill, J.S. (1844, II.2–5).

[25] Mill, J.S. (1844, second essay).

of structural crisis has disappeared,[26] with the result that the serious, prolonged structural crises of the 1930s and 1980s and the crisis of 2008–2018 are still being analysed with the inadequate tool of the business cycle.

And yet, towards the end of the nineteenth century things had already come to a head. While it was celebrating the peace and well-being of the Belle Époque, Europe slumped into a long depression that continued up to the First World War. Only a few authors realised that the depression was caused by the structural imbalance between supply, that is production, and demand, that is consumption (see Sect. 5.1.1). Not even the second Industrial Revolution—in the second half of the nineteenth century—sufficed to absorb the excess of surplus.

This goes to show that Industrial Revolution, or in other words episodes of rapid burgeoning of many productive innovations, eventually aggravate the problem if they occur in a context of low wages. In fact, thanks to technical progress, productivity, and with it the surplus, increase rapidly while the final demand lags behind. Such was the case analysed by Keynes in the 1930s. In the short run, the increase in surplus is absorbed by the new investments; in the medium period it is absorbed by the increase of the middle classes; but in the long term, if there is no increase in wages, it no longer finds any outlet.

This is precisely what happened at the end of the nineteenth century. While the surplus grew, the streets of Europe were stained with the blood of striking workers, denied any increase in wages. The First World War seemed to put an end to the economic depression, absorbing the surplus in armaments and armies. But this was only a truce. As the First World War came to an end, the countries of Europe and the USA were invaded by the unemployed. Development failed to rally due to the persisting want of demand. Left with no outlet, capital was diverted towards financial speculation. Unemployment and inflation took their toll on the less protected middle classes, horrified at the prospect of sinking into the proletariat.[27]

The stage was set for the Wall Street crash of 1929 and the re-emergence of depression which, going from bad to worse, was called stagnation. The levels of consumption and wages have remained the essential factors in all the cases of crisis and development in the last hundred years.

[26] Reference to Perrotta (2018, ch. XIII). However, Minsky's point of view is different from that of the economic cycle: see Roncaglia (2019, 11.6: 1161–1167).

[27] Bairoch (1997, ch. XXIV.3).

References

Bairoch, Paul (1997) *Storia economica e sociale del mondo*, trans. of *Victoires et déboires. Histoire économique et sociale du monde du XVIe siècle à nos jours*, Torino: Einaudi, 1999.

Barton, John (1817) *Observations on … the Conditions of the Labouring Classes …*, Baltimore: Johns Hopkins Univ., 1934.

Bold, Tessa, Molina, E. and Safir, A. (2017) *Clientelism in the Public Sector*, Background Paper for *World Development Report 2017*, online.

Cantillon, Richard (1730) *Essai sur la nature du commerce en général*, London: Macmillan, 1931 (also English text).

Defoe, Daniel (1728) *Plan of the English Commerce…*, reprint, New York: Kelley, 1967.

Ferguson, Adam (1767) *Saggio sulla storia della società civile*, Firenze: Vallecchi, 1973, trans. from English.

Furniss, Edgar (1920) *The Position of the Laborer in a System of Nationalism*, reprint, New York: Delley, 1965.

Gilboy, Elizabeth (1936) "The Cost of Living and Real Wages in Eighteenth Century England", *Review of Economics and Statistics*, August: 134–143.

Janssen, Theodore (1713) *General Maxims in Trade…*, in *The British Merchant* (1713, I: 1–21).

Malthus, Thomas Robert (1820) *Principles of Political Economy*, 2nd ed. London: Pickering, 1836, online Google from Bodleian Library, Oxford.

Marx, Karl, *Capital I* (1867), trans. from German, Moscow: Progress Publishers, www.marxists.org/archive.

Mill, James (1808) *Commerce Defended*, London: Baldwin, online Library of Liberty.

Mill, John Stuart (1844) *Essays on Some Unsettled Questions of Political Economy*, 2nd ed. 1874, London: Longmans, online Library of Economics & Liberty.

OWD (Our World in Data), ed. Max Roser, online https://ourworldindata.org/.

Perrotta, Cosimo (2018) *Unproductive Labour in Political Economy*, London and New York: Routledge.

Polanyi, Karl, et al. (1957) *Traffici e mercati negli antichi imperi*, trans. from English, Torino: Einaudi, 1978.

Ricardo, David (1820) *Notes on Malthus' "Principles of Political Economy"*, J. Hollander and T. Gregory, eds., Baltimore: Johns Hopkins Press.

——— (1821) *Principles of Political Economy and Taxation*, London: Murray, online: Library of Economics & Liberty.

Roncaglia, Alessandro (2019) *L'età della disgregazione. Storia del pensiero economico contemporaneo*, Bari and Roma: Laterza, ebook.

Say, Jean-Baptiste (1803) *Traité d'économie politique*, 6th ed. Paris: Guillaumin, 1841, online Inst. Coppet.

Schultz, Theodore (1961) "Investment in Human Capital", *The American Economic Review*, March: 1–17.
Schumpeter, Joseph A. (1911) *The Theory of Economic Development*, trans. from German, Cambridge, MA: Harvard UP, 1949.
Sismondi, Charles (1819) *Nouveaux principes d'économie politiques*, 2a ed. 1827, Paris: Delaunay, 2 vol., online I tome: Gallica, BNF; II tome: Univ. of Michigan.
Smith, Adam (1776) *Wealth of Nations*, E. Cannan, ed. London: Methuen, 1904, online Library of Economics & Liberty.
Sombart, Werner (1912) *Luxury and Capitalism*, trans. from German, Ann Arbor: Univ. of Michigan Press, 1967.
Sweezy, Paul (1981) *Four Lectures on Marxism*, New York and London: Monthly Review Press.
Tanenbaum, Morris (1983a) *Automation*, entry of *The New Encyclopaedia Britannica*, 15th ed., 1983, vol. 2: 505–514.
——— (1983b) *Mass Production*, entry of *The New Encyclopaedia Britannica*, 15th ed., 1983, vol. 11: 595–600.
Torrens, Robert (1819) *Mr. Owen's Plans for Relieving the National Distress*, in Id., *The Economists Refuted …*, P. Groenewegen, ed., Univ. of Sydney, 1984.
Veblen, Thorstein (1899) *The Theory of the Leisure Class*, online moglen.law.columbia.edu.
Wallerstein, Immanuel (1995) *Capitalismo storico e civiltà capitalistica*, trans. from English, Trieste: Asterios, 2000.

CHAPTER 4

Plundering the World

Abstract The European capitalist countries embarked open conquest of the world to draw on all kinds of resources including precious minerals, and to have the use of slave labour. The history of colonialism shows a long series of atrocities including genocide of indigenous populations in much of the conquered world. Theories on the causes of imperialism/colonialism offer useful but insufficient explanations. Colonialism did not export European civilisation, as is still claimed, but generated extreme exploitation and monoculture. This is still making it very difficult for the ex-colonies to shake off the financial and commercial exploitation practised by the rich countries (neo-colonialism).

Keywords Plunder • Genocides • Colonialism • Neo-colonialism • International trade

Calchi Novati and Valsecchi write: "The history of the colonial adventure is indistinguishable from the history of accumulation of capital".[1] In the fifteenth century the countries of Western Europe set about exploration and conquest of the rest of the world. The conquest was accomplished mainly in two forms. The first was colonialism in the strict sense, that is military subjugation of the other peoples, with which the conquerors cohabit. The second is transference of groups of Europeans to relatively

[1] Calchi Novati and Valsecchi (2016, 6.3: 188).

© The Author(s) 2020

C. Perrotta, *Is Capitalism Still Progressive?*,
https://doi.org/10.1007/978-3-030-48169-8_4

thinly populated areas, almost always accompanied by genocide of the native population. By the end of the nineteenth century the conquest of the world was practically complete.

Marx (*Capital I*) discussed the primitive, or original, accumulation of wealth that constituted the necessary basis for capitalism to take off. He distinguished between a process of primitive accumulation within Europe and an external process. The former accomplished the concentration of capital which was expropriated from the independent producers and small entrepreneurs (ch. 26), while the latter consisted in the acquisition of wealth from other parts of the world (ch. 27). Ghosh (2017) rightly observed that the external process of primitive accumulation has never ceased to function.

4.1 The Plunder of Africa and the Slave Trade

Around 1420, urged on by Prince Henry the Navigator, son of the king, the Portuguese began exploration of the western coast of Africa. In 1488 Bartolomeu Dias rounded the Cape of Good Hope and in 1498 Vasco da Gama reached India by sea. The Portuguese set up a series of fortified cities along the African coast which served as bases for trade and centres for the sorting of raw materials gathered in the hinterland (within a range of about a hundred kilometres from the coast). Gold was the main item, but also ivory, fine woods, precious stones and coffee. The sixteenth century saw new trade bases added by the British, Dutch, French and Danish.[2]

The slave trade—already pursued in Africa by Arabs and Portuguese—began in the sixteenth century in the direction of the Americas. At first, the Portuguese and Spaniards bought the war slaves of certain local kingdoms; subsequently, with the complicity of a number of tribes, they captured millions of men in the western coastal area and took them to the Americas to toil in the mines and on the plantations. The eighteenth century saw the beginning of the cotton plantations with slaves in the south of the USA.[3] The traffickers were merchants from all over Western Europe, including Italians, Danes and Germans, as well as the India Companies of various states that obtained contracts from Spain or Portugal in exchange for a tax.

[2] Calchi Novati and Valsecchi (2016, 4.2: 109–111).

[3] On slavery in the USA, see Genovese (1965, chs. 1 and 2).

The trade peaked in the eighteenth century, after which it began to decline due to reproduction of the slaves in America and the formation of families (less costly than the trade), and indeed the fact that with economic development the trade was no longer sufficiently advantageous. The slaves were transported in inhuman conditions, apparently only a third of the men arriving at their destinations alive.

During the Enlightenment a cultural critique of the trade also developed, plunging it into crisis in the nineteenth century.[4] Progressively, as from the end of the eighteenth century, the slave trade (but not slavery itself) was abolished, although Portugal and Spain were still engaged in it after the mid-nineteenth century. It has been estimated that 10 or 12 million slaves arrived in America alive.[5] This had devastating economic consequences for Africa, also in terms of demographic decline.

In the sixteenth century the Portuguese settled in Angola to hunt down slaves, and indeed in Mozambique. The French carried out de facto occupation of Senegal and Madagascar, to be followed by Algeria in the mid-nineteenth century. In the course of the centuries, the various European states—and the Arabs on the eastern coast—went through conquest and loss of territories and cities, fighting amongst themselves. By the end of the nineteenth century, most of Africa was dominated through private companies, often enjoying monopolies. It was a period that saw European states forcing treaties on the local governments to their detriment, and to the advantage of the companies.[6] So it was that spices, cotton, coffee, cacao, bananas and above all precious metals found their way to Europe.

Armed conquest was generalised only when the local communities tried to rebel against the treaties forced on them. The last two decades of the nineteenth century saw Africa totally divided up (except for Ethiopia and Liberia) amongst the French, British, Portuguese, German, Belgians and Italians. The wars that ensued on colonial conquest to suppress the rebellions led to further demographic decline. Even direr demographic consequences came with the brutal exploitation of the workers—as in the Congo and German South West Africa—inflicted by the mining and timber companies. Brutal massacres also occurred in the war of the British against the rebels in Tanganyika and Somaliland, and in the Italian repression in Cyrenaica and elsewhere.

[4] See e.g. Perdices and Ramos (2017). Pisanelli (2018: 109–181).

[5] Calchi Novati and Valsecchi (2016, 4.2: 116).

[6] Calchi Novati and Valsecchi (2016, 6.2: 182–184).

The horrors perpetrated from 1885 to 1908 in the so-called free state of the Congo were so extreme that even colonialist Europe, accustomed to brutality, eventually found them intolerable. The Belgian King Leopold II had obtained the Congo as his private property, "to bring civilisation" and "fight slavery". His ally, the famous explorer Henry M. Stanley, extorted from the tribal chiefs agreement on contracts to produce ivory, gold, diamonds, rubber and other plants. The hunting of elephants and other wildlife was freely encouraged; villages were destroyed to make room for crops to be exported, and the natives were reduced to slavery. Those who failed to produce the huge quotas of produce assigned came in for appalling mutilation, and their wives and children were set to do their work. Rebellion meant death. The resulting number of dead has been estimated at between three and ten million. The Belgian Parliament finally removed the Congo from the king's private administration, but the whipping and mutilation still went on. Leopold II managed to stop news of his crimes emerging, destroying all the evidence so successfully that even now true knowledge of the facts remains very limited.[7]

4.2 The Colonial Plunder of Latin America

The Spanish conquest of America followed the pattern of the *Reconquista* against the Arabs, which had been led by the feudal nobility and completed in the same year as the discovery of the New World. The economic-social model exported was not capitalist but feudal, with tremendously heavy consequences for Latin America still visible today.

As from 1510, in small numbers with scant means, the Spanish and other European adventurers destroyed vast empires thanks to their technical superiority. They had horses, firearms, steel and the wheel, all of which the natives lacked, and they were expert in military strategy. The *Indios* were decimated, above all by the epidemics (caused by the new germs brought by the Europeans and favoured by urbanisation),[8] and then by slave labour in the mines and plantations, the massacres of war and, finally, the destruction of their economic systems. According to recent calculations, when the Spanish arrived the population of Latin America stood at around 50 million, but by 1650 it had fallen to 10 million.[9]

[7] Stockton (2018).
[8] Ostler (2015: 3–6).
[9] Bairoch (1997, ch. XVIII.2.a).

Having plundered the gold and gems in the possession of the natives, the Spanish went on to exploit the huge deposits of gold, silver and precious stones. It is now estimated that in the sixteenth to eighteenth centuries more than 112,000 tonnes of precious metals found their way to Europe, calculating gold in the silver equivalent: it was worth 15 times the same quantity of silver (ibid.: 763).

Slave labour was extended to the great plantations exporting tropical produce to Europe. Together with sugarcane (the principal export), fine woods, spices and, later, cotton and coffee were also exported. Then there were the crops unknown in the Old World, including cacao, tobacco, potatoes, manioc and tomatoes. Work on the plantations activated the traffic of African slaves, mainly to the Caribbean, Brazil, Venezuela and Colombia. Slave labour was in fact so cheap that it was preferred to industrial production. About 95% of the European trade in African slaves went to Latin America, and 5% to the south of the USA.[10]

The productive structure was based on the *encomienda* system, by which the sovereign granted the Spanish settlers a certain number of *Indios*. In exchange for "protection" and "civilisation", that is forced conversion to Christianity, the natives had to pay tributes in gold, in kind or in work. A part of these tributes went to the sovereign. A similar system was set up in Brazil, but with explicit permission to reduce the *Indios* to slavery.

In the eighteenth century the *encomienda* system fell into decline because Spain—ever poorer due to the reckless economic policy embarked upon in the sixteenth century (see Sect. 2.2.4)—raised the share of earnings that was to go to the sovereign to an excessive degree. With the new *hacienda* system, the *Indios* were formally free but in practice bound to the land by debts (ibid.: 768–769). Gold and silver production increased together with the produce of the plantations thanks to the policy of the first Bourbons of Spain, making the administrative system less oppressive and encouraging the enterprise of the local governors. All this increased the exploitation of the colonial resources.

4.3 Exploitation of the Asian Countries

In the sixteenth century the Portuguese conquered Goa (India), Colombo (Ceylon), the state of Malacca and finally Macao in China. Towards the end of the century, in Burma, they massacred most of the capital's

[10] Bairoch (1997, ch. XX.1.b).

population. In keen competition with the Portuguese, Holland occupied Java in the early years of the seventeenth century, and then all of what is now Indonesia. The latter became a colony early in the nineteenth century when great plantations of coffee, sugarcane and tea were created, together with mining activities. The (forced) labour conditions were so dire as to arouse the indignation of Dutch public opinion. Ceylon (now Sri Lanka), too, was subsequently taken over by the Portuguese, Dutch and, finally, British for the cultivation of coffee and tea—as well as rubber in the twentieth century—for export.

The Philippines were discovered in 1521 by Magalhães (Magellan), who was in the service of Spain. The Spanish introduced the *encomienda* system there, but subsequently the state assigned the lands directly to religious orders and nobles. The natives were subjected to fierce exploitation. The Chinese immigrants suffered a series of massacres by the dominators and were expelled in the eighteenth century. The nineteenth century saw extension of the range of crops for export (hemp, sugar and copra). At the end of the nineteenth century the Spanish gave way to the USA and the Philippines became America's major source of sugar.

Greater difficulties were faced in the conquest of Southeast Asia, where ancient civilisations flourished. Only Thailand remained independent, deftly playing on the rivalry between British and French. Burma was subdued by the British after no fewer than three wars, and was associated with the Indian colony, to share its fate. Liberation from the British came in 1948. As for Indochina (Vietnam, Laos and Cambodia), the French occupied Saigon in 1859, but the actual war of conquest lasted from 1883 to 1896. The plantations set up by the French exported rubber, sugar, coconuts, rice and raw cotton. The mines, under the control of the Western companies, exported coal and zinc.

At the beginning of the twentieth century Korea became a colony of Japan, which had by then achieved industrialisation. From then on it exported mainly rice, coal, iron and fertilisers for the Japanese. The living conditions and wages of the Koreans deteriorated miserably, and suppression of the revolts was ruthless.

The commercial enterprises of many European states had found their way into the rich India of the Mogul Empire. Portuguese, Dutch, Danish, French and British all set up their bases there. In the eighteenth century, with the progressive decline of the Mogul dynasty the competition between the European states waxed keener, until the French and British remained in dominant positions. With the victory of Plassey (in 1757) against the French and Indians of Calcutta, the British embarked upon domination as a protectorate, which extended to the whole of India in 1818. In the following hundred years the liberalisation of trade imposed by the British ruined India's flourishing cotton textile industry, the British industry being vastly more productive thanks to mechanisation. It was much the same story for the iron and steel industry, and even for agriculture.

In the mid-eighteenth century export of Indian manufactures to England by far exceeded the imports from that country, but by the end of the nineteenth century the situation had reversed. India was exporting raw materials, including raw cotton, and importing manufactures. Thus the typical pattern of colonial domination was achieved. Today 60% of India's population is active in the agricultural sector,[11] which is indicative of extreme backwardness.

The nineteenth century saw China set on a downward path. In the mid-eighteenth century this great country had practically shut out trade with the West, which was now allowed only in Canton and under state supervision. However, the British continued to obtain precious Chinese goods (silk, porcelain, spices, agricultural produce, textiles and so forth) illegally in exchange for the clandestine supply of opium.

China rose up against the introduction of opium twice (the Opium Wars, 1839–1842 and 1858), but lost to the military superiority of the British, and subsequently of the French, too. At the end of the century it was Japan that now turned on China, occupying Taiwan. Eventually, besides Hong Kong the British succeeded in securing the opening of many Chinese ports, as well as consent for the opium traffic, permission for the Europeans to bear arms, and even general control of the customs.

The negative results of reducing China to a virtual colony soon became evident. Bairoch speaks of nothing less than deindustrialisation, albeit less drastic than in the case of India thanks to the staunch resistance of the bureaucracy and the industrial modernisation that had been launched in the 1870s. Nevertheless, by 1910 only 70% of control of the Chinese textile industry was in local hands. While the Chinese accounted for 26% of

[11] Sideri (2010: 78).

the total world population, the country possessed only 0.6% of the world's spinning plants and 0.2% of the iron and steel industry. However, looking to the example set by Japan the country made a great endeavour to catch up with the West, including foundation of many universities.[12]

4.4 Genocide in the "Sparsely Populated" Lands

It is true that some of the worst cases of genocide perpetrated in the world in the last century had nothing to do with capitalism and the associated colonisation. This applies to the Turkish genocide of the Armenians, the Nazi genocide of Jews and gypsies, the Stalinist genocides, those of the Khmer Rouge, and on to the Tutsi in Rwanda and the Rohingya in Myanmar (Burma). However, the colonial genocides have remained to a considerable extent unknown and underestimated because they have been kept hidden. Here we will recall only the major cases.

It is often held that with colonisation the total or virtual disappearance of the natives was an inevitable consequence. Actually, the extinction has almost always been deliberate, planned by the white colonists. The driving force of European expansion derived from the development of capitalism, but the genocides were certainly not necessary. Even if imposed, expansion could have been conducted peacefully, leaving the land necessary for survival to the indigenous population. This would have amounted to a great advantage for the Europeans, too. Today, the genocides of colonisation are at last being exposed through a number of studies.[13]

Often the colonised lands had been thinly populated compared with Europe because the natives depended above all on hunting and gathering, and so needed particularly extensive territories. Such was the case of Northern America, Amazonia and the Southern Cone of America, as well as the Kalahari and Congo in Africa, the aborigines in Australia and many small aboriginal populations in Asia and Oceania.

* * *

As for North America, it is estimated that between 5 and 10 million natives were living in the area now occupied by the USA when the white men arrived, but by 1900 they had dwindled to 300,000. In New England the

[12] Bairoch (1997: 873–880).

[13] See the references in Rensing (2011: 25–36).

first settlers believed that America was their promised land. As Roy Crazy Horse put it, "The claim that the land was empty was followed by a determined effort to make it empty".[14] In 1630 the Massachusetts Bay Colony declared shooting illegal, except at Indians and wolves (ibid.: 28). In 1636–1638, together with some local tribes the British settlers massacred the Pequot tribe and scattered the survivors.[15] The French, too, engaged in wholesale slaughter in the course of their wars against the native populations, targeting in particular the Natchez.[16]

According to Ostler, the mission of the settlers was territorial expansion, both to enrich themselves and because they believed that only private property guaranteed freedom. Thus they decided to demand that the Indians should give up their lands in exchange for "civilisation". When the Indians refused, they could only fall back on war of extermination.

So it was that in 1779 George Washington, the hero of the war for independence, proclaimed the objective of "total destruction and devastation of their settlements" in dealing with the Iroquois. In 1798 the Minister of War, Henry Knox, ordered the army to "extirpate, utterly, if possible" the confederated Indians of Ohio. In 1807 President Jefferson, one of the founding fathers of the constitution, threatened the same treatment for the Indians in the area of Detroit. Ostler commented that "America was born fighting Indians".

In 1851, with the goldrush underway, the governor of California declared a "war of extermination… until the Indian race becomes extinct". The Yuki children were reduced to slavery. And when the Yuki and Yanas, denied any chance of hunting, killed the settlers' cattle, the settlers formed squads to kill the Indians systematically, with the support of the governor. In California, in the space of a mere 12 years (1848–1860) the Indian population fell from 150,000 to 30,000. Besides direct slaughter, diseases and famine brought on by the conditions of forced labour and the loss of their land also played their part.[17] The state and federal government spent over $1,700,000 on extermination of the Indians in California.

The massacres perpetrated in the so-called *Indian wars* reached staggering numbers, often carried out in cold blood. At Sand Creek in 1864

[14] Chief Roy (2002: 25–26).
[15] Rensing (2011: 30–32). Ostler (2015: 7–8).
[16] Cesa (1994: 260a).
[17] Ostler (2015: 9–13).

the governor of Colorado ordered that a great number of Cheyenne and Arapaho, including women and children, be killed in their sleep. In many areas squads were formed, on the initiative of or tacitly accepted by the authorities, to set about systematically hunting down and killing the Indians. Other massacres were organised directly by the settlers. The Indians in the territory of the USA were also subjected to sterilisation, expulsion from their territories and reduction to slavery with seizure of their land.[18]

Besides the direct massacres, genocide was also carried out by seizing the vital resources—not only their land, but also their bison. Buffalo Bill acquired that name and fame for his victory in a competitive "hunt" for bison, which was in reality a massacre. Apparently he killed over 4000 between 1868 and 1872. Once the Indians had been confined to the reserves, which they were forbidden to leave, driven by hunger they would make their way out and attack the homes of the settlers, to be met with yet further massacres. The slaughter went on even when the last of the tribes had been defeated with the excuse of false or deliberately created incidents, as in the case of the massacre of Wounded Knee (in 1890), where 300 Indians—mostly women and children—fell under machine-gun fire. Killing children was a major objective, with the aim of obliterating the very existence of the Indians.

In Canada the mid-nineteenth century saw the introduction of a state plan to take away the Indians' land and natural resources. *The plan is still in force*. Children were taken away from their mothers to be sent to the western schools. Canada's Indians are still confined in reserves today. Like the aborigines of Australia, many pass the time getting drunk in a sort of collective suicide. On 3/6/2019 the Canadian government expressed contrition for having killed over 1000 native women between 1980 and 2012 (news in the media of 4/6/2019).

* * *

The picture was also grim in South America. In British Guiana the colonists seized the land of the natives in the 1960s to take possession of the gold and diamonds. In Colombia, in the year 2000, the U'wa tribe,

[18] Rensing (2011: 19–21 and 26).

having already been robbed of 85% of its territory, lost yet more territory because it was rich in oil. The wells were protected by Colombian troops in the pay of Occidental Petroleum (California).[19]

In Argentina fake news spread that the natives were facing extinction, and that their disappearance was a natural process.[20] As compensation for the colonists' occupation of the land, treaties were drawn up with the natives, only to be violated, and the natives massacred. In 1878–1885 a military campaign was conducted for the white colonists to expand over the pampas and into Patagonia. The campaign was called "Conquest of the Desert", to give the impression that no one was living in those immense regions (inhabited by Indians).[21]

In November 1878, at Villa Mercedes, the Ranquel asked for the "rations" of food promised with the newly signed treaty, and were massacred in response, the women and children being put to forced labour. In 1883 the army attacked the camp of the Inacayal and slaughtered everyone there, including the women and children. At the end of the "war" the Indians were concentrated in camps and reduced to slavery; the children were taken from their mothers, and the women were turned into sex slaves. The appalling living conditions served to bring about the destruction of the Indian tribes.

Today in the schools of Argentina the pupils are taught that the Indians no longer exist. The few survivors, like the Mapuche, are classified as foreigners in accordance with the plan to render the Indians invisible. Again, in 1947, under Perón, a campaign of genocide was launched against the Pilagá, guilty of having gathered to pray with the shaman because they were dying of hunger. Extermination has continued to the present day. From 1994 to 2007, in the province of Chaco, the land under public property (the only land on which the Indians can live, being denied any private property) was reduced from 3.5 million to 650,000 hectares.[22]

In Chile the Mapuche resisted the Spanish invasion until they obtained independence of their territory to the south of the river Bío-Bío, but from

[19] Neu and Therrien (2003, Introduction: 1–4).
[20] Delrio et al. (2010: 139).
[21] Trinchero (2006: 125–130).
[22] Delrio et al. (2010: 140–150).

1860 to 1885 independent Chile invaded the territory of the Mapuche and subjugated them alongside the "Conquest of the Desert" in Argentina. The white conquerors deported the native Chileans to the reserves, with attempts to exterminate them or deprive them of their identity. In the 1970s Pinochet issued a law that left the Mapuche with no constitutional guarantees. And even now the Mapuche have no protection against the continual illegal grabbing of their land.[23]

Perhaps the most successful of genocides was perpetrated against the Charrúa in Uruguay. According to the official version, this population disappeared in 1831 and the country now has only a white population. Eliminating identity is an essential part of genocide. In 1831, having gained independence, Uruguay turned treacherously on the natives and exterminated them with three successive attacks. The official propaganda makes no mention of the massacre, but states that the Charrúa do not exist. In the last few years, the 2000 surviving (and hidden) Charrúa have reorganised themselves. Today 5% of the population state that they are indigenous and ask to be recognised. In fact, DNA testing shows that there is a great deal of indigenous blood amongst the residents.[24]

* * *

As for Africa, we have already considered the Congo (Sect. 4.2). In Namibia in 1904–1908 the German settlers massacred 80% of the hundred thousand Herero to take over their land and capital. The other Herero were driven to the desert, where the Germans had blocked the wells.[25]

* * *

In Australia the aborigines, who numbered well over a million in 1788 (the year of discovery) had dwindled to a few thousand by the beginning of the twentieth century, decimated by the diseases brought by the Europeans. Nevertheless, faced with soil low on fertility the colonists occupied countless portions of land. Deprived of their land, the

[23] Mariqueo and Calbucura (2002).
[24] Albarenga (2017).
[25] See the article by Norimitsu Onishi, *New York Times*, Dec. 29, 2016.

aborigines—who were hunter-gatherers—had to settle for the sheep and the fruit grown by the colonisers. They had no idea of private property. And they were regularly killed by the colonists, in great numbers. For the colonists this was a simple matter of routine. In the 1830s the authorities drew up a list of rewards for every aborigine killed: 5 pounds for an adult, 2 pounds for a child, in both Australia and Tasmania (a similar practice obtained in the Southern Cone of America in the twentieth century). Thus slaughter practically became a sport.

Under pressure from the British government, in 1838 some white settlers guilty of having killed some aborigines in cold blood were tried and sentenced to death. Since then the aborigines have been gathered together in reserves. Government committees decided whether to grant them permission to travel or get married, assigning their work, homes and the missionaries to convert them. The children were taken away from their parents, sent to English schools and punished if they spoke their own language. Apparently there were many cases of violence and sexual abuse, never punished. The aborigines' culture has almost completely disappeared and they are prey to alcoholism and depression.[26]

In Tasmania, Colonel George Arthur put into circulation fake news about the aggressiveness of the aborigines and the good will of the government to come to peaceful agreements, extermination presented as inevitable war. The massacres were covered by military secret, but the records show that the genocide had been planned from the outset. From 1824 to the mid-1830s the aborigines dwindled from several thousand to a few dozen and fled to the nearby islands. In 1905 the last representative of the aborigine population died, and with her the time-honoured culture and language of that people.[27]

* * *

The cultural genocide was, then, no less serious than the massacres. In the USA a system was created between the late nineteenth and early twentieth century to destroy the native culture through the children. The idea was "Kill the Indian, Save the Man", as stated in 1892 by Richard Henry Pratt,

[26] Stockton (2017).
[27] Harman (2018).

the founder of the school for Indians in Pennsylvania.[28] Between 1879 and 1902, 400 schools were set up for children seized from their parents; they could not speak their language and were forced to give up the beliefs and the very name of their people.

In 2001 it was estimated that there were 200 or 300 million aborigines in the world, almost all of them fighting to defend their land, and almost always losing out. The case of the tribes of Amazonia is well-known and highly topical. Much the same is happening to the Sami in Scandinavia and the Mohawks, Nisga'a and Inuit in Canada, as well as the Maya in Chiapas.[29] Only in the last few years have some institutional representatives begun to admit—grudgingly and generically—the violence inflicted on the indigenous populations and asked for pardon. This has happened in New Zealand, Australia, California, Canada and even in the USA, with an admission by Obama in 2009 that has been more or less hushed up.

4.5 Theories on the Causes of Economic Domination

The history of the colonial conquests belies the idea that the spread of capitalism over the world was due to the natural and peaceful expansion of the capitalistic market. This is the idea that lay behind Ricardo's law of comparative advantages. Ricardo (1821) extended to international trade Smith's theory on the advantages of the division of labour. If, he wrote, every country specialises in the production that costs it least (instead of producing all the goods it needs on its own), each country can trade its products with those of the others to their reciprocal advantage (ch. VII).

Ricardo's law still dominates mainstream economics. Samuelson (1948) proposed it anew using the three factors of production (land, labour and capital). Every country should find it advantageous to specialise in the factor of production that it has most of (and so is less dear), and obtain through trade products with prevalence of the other factors of production.[30] The nineteenth century saw the first theories alternative to Ricardo's finding formulation. It was observed that capitalist expansion in the world was by no means peaceful or based on reciprocal advantageousness.

[28] Rensing (2011: 23).

[29] Neu and Therrien (2003: 3).

[30] See on this Boianovsky (2019a).

Rather, it was based on the greed of the capitalist élite (Hobson) or on competition amongst the monopolies to dominate (Lenin).[31]

The most controversial of the authors was Rosa Luxemburg, a Marxist with an underconsumption approach, criticised by the orthodox Marxists. According to Luxemburg, the capitalist economy lacked internal demand capable of absorbing the increasing surplus. In fact, wages were blocked at the subsistence level by exploitation, the entrepreneurs were set on reinvesting profits, and the consumption of the middle classes—being unproductive—could not represent an outlet for investment. The only possible outlet, therefore, was investment abroad. However, together with capital the capitalist system itself was also exported, and the foreign populations transformed into new waged workers to exploit. But this brought the same mechanism back into action. Capitalism was driven to seek ever new outlets until, having conquered the whole world, it collapsed for lack of any other outlets.[32]

This analysis does not seem convincing. In the first place, it is not true that a capitalistic economy cannot grow by extending its internal market. Historically, wages have risen and the middle classes and their consumption have increased. Secondly, the vast majority of the financial transfers made by western entrepreneurs to the backward economies do not consist in investment for production but expenditure to obtain the natural resources of those countries.

Equally unconvincing is the theory of Arghiri Emmanuel (1969) that sees the developed countries exploiting the backward ones precisely as the capitalist exploits the waged worker. Actually, it is impossible to see in colonial exploitation the same mechanism of Marxian production of surplus value, which results from the difference between the necessary labour time (which the worker devotes to his own keep) and the surplus labour time (devoted to production of the surplus value, which translates into profit). This hardly has much to do with the exploitation of other countries.

Prebisch (1949) and Singer (1950) come closer to the realities. They start from the decline in prices of raw materials noted by the League of Nations for the period 1870–1930 (although Bairoch contests any such decline).[33] The two authors state that in the trade between manufactures

[31] See Perrotta (2018, ch. IX.5 e XV.4).
[32] Luxemburg (1913, 1915).
[33] Bairoch (1997, ch. XXXV.3.a).

of the rich countries and raw products of the poor countries, the former should cost less than the latter given the substantial increase in productivity shown by western industry, which had reduced their cost. If the contrary case obtained—they held—it was due to the different strength of the unions in the western world, able to exact higher wages. The cost of the west's high wages is discharged on the prices of exports, and the entrepreneurs in the poor countries are in turn forced to offset the increased costs by lowering the workers' wages.

In reality international trade has never shown an advantage in productive capacity translating into a disadvantage in trade, as Prebisch and Singer had hypothesised, but quite the contrary, because the terms of trade are determined by the overall strength of the economies engaging in trade. As Singer himself had pointed out, the prices are determined by the fact that the poor countries absolutely need to export if they are to survive, while there is no such urgency for the rich countries.[34] Of course, over the long period a backward economy will lose out in this trade because the raw materials it exports cannot be used at home to launch development. This creates a vicious circle, which explains why many ex-colonies fail to develop and continue to export the same natural resources as before.[35]

The 1940s saw the birth of development economics, conceived to analyse these perverse processes (which official economics still sees as marginal anomalies), but the only version of this line of study that had much success approached the issue in terms of painless transition from a backward economy to capitalism (see Rostow 1960). On the other hand, Arthur Lewis (1954) proposed industrialisation as an effective response to the mechanism penalising the poor countries. In these countries, Lewis writes, there is widespread hidden unemployment (excess of employed) in agriculture, which keeps the wages very low. The workers in excess could be employed in industry, but on the same wages as before. This would give the poor countries a competitive advantage.[36]

In the 1960s these countries tried to follow Lewis's model with the import substitution policy, or in other words producing at home the industrial products they had been importing from the West (the same strategy had been successfully adopted in the mercantilist policies of the

[34] See Perrotta (2016). See also the other essays by Sunna and Gualerzi (2016).
[35] See e.g. Myrdal (1957) and Balogh (1960).
[36] See the analysis by Boianovsky (2019b).

seventeenth century). But nothing came of it. Stanovnik (1964) demonstrated with detailed documentation that the rich countries refused to import the industrial products of the poor countries, forcing them to remain as exporters of tropical agricultural produce and raw materials (for the use of western industry). Eventually the old international division of labour imposed by the West was restored. At best the poor countries could export industrial assembly components, thanks to which the rich countries could use to their own advantage the low wages of the poor countries, which still came short of industrialisation, burdened with huge financial debts which placed them at the mercy of the rich countries.

4.6 The Heritage of Colonialism and Neo-colonialism

Thanks to Napoleon's invasion of Spain, all the great countries of Latin America were able to win independence in the first decades of the nineteenth century. The Asian and African colonies achieved independence between the end of the Second World War and the 1960s at the cost of fierce struggles. And yet most of the ex-colonies are still far from enjoying economic independence. Colonialism has given way to neo-colonialism, through which the West's economic domination continues along two lines: control of the international financial and trade mechanisms on the one hand, and alliance with the local elites and corruption on the other.

The former colonial powers support the legend that colonialism had worked to the advantage of the colonies because it introduced the techniques and culture of the West. But the fact is that colonial domination proved economically devastating for these countries. The capitalist countries had gone on grabbing resources from all the other countries for over five centuries without actually exporting the system of capitalistic production, except for the countries where the white settlers had taken the place of the indigenous population.

Colonialism has left very little in terms of modern infrastructure, essentially that which served for exploitation of the mines or plantations. On the other hand, it has imposed monoculture (or mono-mining), implying organisation of the entire economy around one or very few products to export to the West.[37] This has destroyed the old subsistence economy, impoverished the social fabric and driven out masses of ex-peasants, artisans and small tradesmen to end up in enormous, chaotic urban conglomerations devoid of services. On top of this, subsequent to independence many countries have had to retain their monoculture, unable to survive without exporting their raw materials.

Observing the ex-colonies today we cannot speak of backwardness but rather of underdevelopment, that is an economy to some extent modernised but distorted and dominated.[38] The mechanisms behind the growing gap can be neutralised only with social and political reforms for long-period development,[39] but the rich countries are doing all they can to stop them from happening. Through the International Monetary Fund and World Bank, which they control, the rich countries lend money to the poor ones on condition that they balance their accounts with drastic cuts in social spending (but not, of course, in the landowners' rents).[40] On top of all this there is now western dumping in agricultural produce. Thanks to public funding, American and EU farms export their produce below market value to Africa and Latin America, sabotaging even the attempts at bottom-up development of the traditional economy of these areas.[41]

Today, as yesterday, the rich countries are still corrupting the elites of the poor countries to be able to exploit their natural resources; they prop up the oppressive dictatorship of kleptomaniac rulers, supporting the middle classes that are privileged and largely parasitic in these countries. When the possibility of creating an embryo welfare state for the lower classes has materialised, the middle-upper classes—with the connivance of the West—have reacted with capital flight as well as boycott of the administrative apparatus and essential services, often with death squads in their pay. Thus the lower classes are driven to support social policies even by violating democratic principles while the privileged classes exploit formal democracy to defend their abuses.

Finally, the western multinationals engage in unlimited exploitation of the mineral, oil, agricultural and natural resources of the African countries

[37] See e.g. Brancovic (1959, ch. 2).
[38] See e.g. Furtado (1961).
[39] See Hirschman (1958).
[40] Alacevich (2007).
[41] Guerrieri (2012: 216).

as well as vast areas of Latin America and Asia. To maintain this control they have no qualms about instigating interminable civil wars involving child soldiers or contractors recruited by Western, Russian and Chinese companies.

References

Agarwala, A.N. and Singh, S.P. (eds.) (1958) *The Economics of Underdevelopment*, Oxford University Press, 1963.

Alacevich, Michele (2007) *Le origini della Banca Mondiale*, Milano: Bruno Mondadori.

Albarenga, Pablo (2017) "Where did Uruguay's indigenous population go?", *El País* in English, Nov. 10.

Bairoch, Paul (1997) *Storia economica e sociale del mondo*, trans. of *Victoires et déboires. Histoire économique et sociale du monde du XVIe siècle à nos jours*, Torino: Einaudi, 1999.

Balogh, Thomas (1960) "Investimenti all'interno e investimenti all'estero", in Id., *Una società di ineguali*, trans. of *Unequal Partners*, Torino: Einaudi, 1967: 220–235.

Boianovsky, Mauro (2019a) "Reacting to Samuelson: Early Development Economics and the Factor-Price Equalization Theorem", CHOPE Working Paper No. 2019-11.

——— (2019b) "Arthur Lewis and the Classical Foundations of Development Economics", in *Including a Symposium on 50 Years of the Union for Radical Political Economics*, online.

Brancovic, Slobodan (1959) *Il problema dei paesi sottosviluppati*, Milano: Feltrinelli.

Calchi Novati, Gian Paolo and Valsecchi, Pierluigi (2016) *Africa: la storia ritrovata*, Roma: Carocci.

Cesa, Marco (1994) *Genocidio*, entry of *Enciclopedia delle Scienze sociali*, vol. IV, Roma: Istituto dell'Enciclopedia Italiana.

Chief Roy, Crazy Horse (2002) *The North American Genocide*, Washington: Powathan Press.

Delrio, Walter, Lenton, D., Musante, M., and Nagy, M. (2010) "Discussing Indigenous Genocide in Argentina", *Genocide Studies and Prevention*, 5, 2: 138–159.

Emmanuel, Arghiri (1969) *L'échange inégal*, Paris: Maspero, 1979.

Furtado, Celso (1961) *Teoria dello sviluppo economico*, trans. from French edition, Bari: Laterza, 1972.

Genovese, Eugene (1965) *L'economia politica della schiavitù*, trans. from English, Torino: Einaudi, 1972.

Ghosh, Jayati (2017) "150 years of 'Das Kapital': How Relevant is Marx Today?", *Real-World Economics Review Blog*, August 24, 2017.

Guerrieri, Paolo (2012) "PAC (Politica Agricola Comune)", entry of *Economia e Finanza*, vol. II, Roma: Istituto dell'Enciclopedia Italiana.

Harman, Kristyn (2018) "Explainer: The Evidence for the Tasmanian Genocide", *The Conversation*, Jan. 17.

Hirschman, Albert (1958) *The Strategy of Economic Development*, New York and London: Norton.

Lewis, Arthur W. (1954) *Economic Development with Unlimited Supply of Labour*, *The Manchester School*, Now in Agarwala and Singh (1958): 400–449.

Luxemburg, Rosa (1913) *The Accumulation of Capital*, trans. from German, London: Routledge & Kegan Paul, 1951, online Marxists Archive.

——— (1915) *An Anti-Critique*, trans. from German, 1st ed. 1921, online: Marxists Archive.

Mariqueo, Reynaldo and Calbucura, J. (2002) "The Mapuche Nation", www.mapuche-nation.org, Sept. 2.

Marx, Karl (1867) *Capital I*, trans. from German, Moscow: Progress Publishers.

Myrdal, Gunnar (1957) *Teoria economica e paesi sottosviluppati*, trans. from English, Milano: Feltrinelli, 1966.

Neu, Dean and Therrien, R. (2003) *Accounting for Genocide: Canada's Bureaucratic Assault on Aboriginal People*, Winnipeg, MB: Fernwood Publishing and Zed Books.

Ostler, Jeffrey (2015) *Genocide and American Indian History*, Oxford research Encyclopaedia. American History; online, downloaded March 14, 2019.

Perdices, Luis and Ramos Gorostiza, José L. (2017) "La economía política de la esclavitud ...", *GeoCrítica*, revista electrónica, XXI, 567: 1–42.

Perrotta, Cosimo (2016) "The Brilliant Fifties: International Trade as a Cause of Underdevelopment", in Sunna and Gualerzi (2016): 51–70.

——— (2018) *Unproductive Labour in Political Economy*, London and New York: Routledge.

Pisanelli, Simona (2018) *Condorcet et Adam Smith*, Paris: Garnier.

Prebisch, Raúl (1949) "El desarrollo económico de la América Latina ..." Now in *Desarrollo económico*, 1986, no. 103: 479–502.

Rensing, Brenden (2011) "Genocide of Native Americans", in S. Totten and R.K. Hitchcock, eds., *Genocide of Indigenous Peoples*, vol. 8, New Brunswick and London: Transaction.

Ricardo, David (1821) *Principles of Political Economy and Taxation*, London: Murray, online Library of Economics & Liberty.

Rostow, Walt W. (1960) *The Stages of Economic Growth*, Cambridge: Cambridge University Press, 1990.

Samuelson, Paul A. (1948) "International Trade and the Equalisation of Factor Prices", *The Economic Journal*, 58: 163–184.

Sideri, Sandro (2010) *L'India e gli altri*, ISPI (Istituto di Studi di Politica Internazionale), online.
Singer, Hans W. (1950) "The Distribution of Gains between Investing and Borrowing Countries", *American Economic Review*, 40: 473–485, from JSTOR.
Stanovnik, Janez (1964) *I paesi in via di sviluppo nell'economia mondiale*, trans. from Serbo-Croatian, Milano: Feltrinelli, 1965.
Stockton, Richard (2017) "Australia's Centuries-Long Genocide Against Aboriginal People", *History Science News*, online, Aug. 15.
——— (2018) "Why Isn't Belgium's King Leopold II As Reviled As Hitler Or Stalin?", *History Science News*, online, Oct. 17.
Sunna, Claudia and Gualerzi, Davide, eds. (2016) *Development Economics in the XXI Century*, Abingdon, UK and New York: Routledge.
Trinchero, Héctor H. (2006) "The Genocide of Indigenous Peoples in the Formation of the Argentine Nation-State", *Journal of Genocide Research*, 8, 2: 121–135.

CHAPTER 5

The Welfare State and Its Crisis

Abstract The welfare state represents the greatest investment in human capital ever made in history, as the data show. It advanced beyond underconsumption and, for the first time, extended well-being to the whole of society. But the 1980s saw the prevalence of parasitic tendencies; instead of moving on to a full post-industrial economy, the eventual outcome was saturation of demand. On top of the unemployment caused by saturation came further unemployment generated by the ICT revolution and then by globalisation, which shifted western manufactures to the emerging countries. From this profound crisis of the West neoliberalism was born, leading to monstrous inequalities. Neoliberalism reasserted the despotism of profit but went on to see rent triumphing once again.

Keywords Post-industrial economy • Saturation • Digital revolution • Globalisation • Profit • Neoliberalism

5.1 The Welfare State Revolution

5.1.1 Overcoming Underconsumption

The distance of a century lies between the Chartist movement (see Sect. 2.1.2) and the crisis of the 1930s, analysed by Keynes. These were years that saw factory workers and farmhands fighting fiercely against starvation wages. It was precisely low wages that led to underconsumption, the

© The Author(s) 2020

C. Perrotta, *Is Capitalism Still Progressive?*,
https://doi.org/10.1007/978-3-030-48169-8_5

consequent lack of demand and thus the drift towards depression (see Sect. 3.4).

At the end of the nineteenth century Loria devised the concept of unproductive capital, stating that when capital does not find uses that produce profit, it tends to create unproductive uses under the guise of investment. Shortly after, Hobson accused the capitalists of avoiding innovative investments based on growth of human capital, thereby bringing about underconsumption. Finally, the Marxist Kautsky (1902) argued that concentration of capital and low wages drove capitalism towards stagnation and increasing impoverishment of the masses.[1] On the other hand, as we have seen (Sect. 2.2.4), orthodox economic theory came up with the contrary interpretation of the growing difficulties of accumulation, holding that the unions stood in the way of the "natural" downward trend of wages. Contesting this thesis, Keynes called for higher wages and increased employment as a way out of the crisis.

With the help of Keynes's theory, in the 1960s—after a thousand years of economic growth—all the social classes including the lowest were at last admitted to enjoy the increase in wealth that capitalistic accumulation generates. This, however, applies—albeit with marked inequalities—to Western Europe and only in part the USA, the other Anglo-Saxon countries and Japan, the vast majority of humanity remaining left out.

The true "great leap ahead" of the 1960s came not in the China of Mao—a dramatic failure—but in Europe. In the aftermath of the Second World War, unlike that of the First, unemployment did not endlessly stagnate but was rapidly absorbed, industrial employment opening up to great masses of population from the most backward rural areas. In Europe, tens of millions of poor farmhands and unemployed poured from the Mediterranean areas into the industrial regions of the Centre-North.[2] The wages of the newcomers were low, weighing down on the wage level of the other workers. To start with, therefore, wages did not increase in level but in number.

The states invested directly in energy sources and key raw materials—including mining, electrification, oil refining, the iron and steel industry and basic chemicals (see e.g. the European Coal and Steel Community)—as well as major infrastructure and transport. A great development of

[1] Loria (1889, vol. I: 400–476; vol. II: 342–372). Hobson (1894, chs. 9, 11, 13, 17). Kautsky (1902: 271–296).

[2] See Van Mol and de Valk (2016).

industry in all the countries of Europe was launched on this basis. The states—even the USA, a shrine of laissez-faire—organised and financed basic research and the new inventions that came to be utilised by the enterprises.[3]

At the same time all the social services that raised the level of the workers' well-being were created or enhanced: the national health service, a system of guarantees (paid sick leave, obligatory days off, maternity leave, etc.), compulsory education up to the age of 14, public housing and subsidised mortgages. A universal pension system was created, and support provided to the unemployed and the weaker categories. Clearly, these measures went beyond the Keynesian logic of increasing employment and raising wages to relaunch investment. Public expenditure became positive investment and growth of human capital. The enterprises benefited enormously from these policies because they created more qualified and efficient labour power.[4] Thus in the age of the welfare state private interest was in accord with solidarity and public interest.

The inflow into the market of great numbers of qualified women (a process that underlay women's liberation) was enabled by modern gas stoves and electrical household appliances, but also by the services supplied by the state. Thanks to obligatory education girls were able to take on jobs other than that of the housewife; the welfare state and national health service to some extent relieved women of the need to look after the elderly and sick at home, while kindergartens, schools and hospitals could lighten the burdens of maternity and child care.

All this led to a long period of expansion lasting 25–30 years. If we compare the 1920s with the 1950s, which had more or less equal starting points, the contrast between the two types of accumulation could not be clearer. In the 1920s the lack of employment policies and social safety nets drove impoverished masses to look to dictatorships of the right or left for protection. On the other hand, as Bairoch demonstrates, the period from 1950 to 1973 saw an unprecedented growth in terms of speed and quantity. Exports grew, too, their volume increasing by 7.4% a year. Moreover, agriculture saw its third revolution, productivity growing fivefold between 1950 and 1990 to surpass the increase in the productivity of industry for the first time.[5]

[3] See Mazzucato (2013, 2018, ch. 7).

[4] For a thesis along these lines, see Lindert (2016: 2–17).

[5] Bairoch (1997, ch. XXV.2).

In the 1960s the workers enjoyed various forms of protection and profits increased thanks to the high consumption of the lower classes rather than miserable wages for the workers. The economy grew, driving up all the factors of development and civilised standards. In a mere 25 years (1950–1975) the developed countries saw life expectancy increased by 10 years, standing between 72 and 75 years.[6] In western Europe the yearly per capita rise in GDP moved on from 2.3% to over 4%, amply surpassing that of the USA, but the period 1970–1990 saw this upward trend slowing down.[7]

There were indeed inequalities, but within reasonable limits, compatible with the criterion of merit, in the period 1950–1970 sinking to their lowest levels in both Europe and the USA. Subsequently, however, they started climbing again.[8] It is to Piketty that we owe perhaps the most apt appraisal of the growth brought about by the welfare state: this was the only period in which, to some extent at least, the principle that we believe in was realised, namely that in a democratic society inequalities depend on merit and not inherited wealth (ibid.: 241).

In the USA the decade 1950–1960 saw a greater percentage increase in wages than in productivity (2.9 as against 2.2), but subsequently the trend reversed until, in 2001–2013, the increase in wages fell to less than a half the increase in productivity (1 against 2.4).[9] However, from 1954 onwards most of the increase in income went to the richest 10% of the population until, in 2009–2012 this 10% appropriated 118% of the increase in income and, naturally, the income of the remaining 90% fell by 18%.[10]

Between 1950 and 1975 the infant mortality rate (under the age of five) fell from about 11% to 2.7% in Europe (and by 2015 it had reached 0.58%).[11] To take the case of an intermediate European country like Germany, the mortality rate of mothers during or after childbirth fell from nearly 184 women per 100,000 children born alive to 27.2 between 1952 and 1979 (and by 2015 it had fallen yet further to 6).[12] In 1947 the daily

[6] OWD, Population—Life expectancy.
[7] See Piketty (2014: 97).
[8] Piketty (2014: 323–324).
[9] Apel (2015: 9).
[10] Tcherneva (2015: 65).
[11] OWD, Population—Child mortality.
[12] OWD, Health—Maternal mortality.

intake of calories in Western Europe stood at around 2300, but by 1975 it had risen to about 3.300.[13]

5.1.2 *Towards the Human Capital (Post-industrial) Economy*

With the welfare state the very nature of accumulation changed. Once underconsumption had been left behind, conditions were created for accumulation of a new type. The new accumulation called for radical transformations if it was to continue development, but the need for this kind of change was not understood. Management of the economy continued as in the past, and this brought an end to the boom, and subsequently a block on growth. In particular, the state had become an indispensable factor for economic progress. Its role was no longer that of emergency measures as in the 1930s, and as even Keynes had contemplated, but policy now needed to be programmed and had to pursue a balance with the private enterprises.

Thanks to the relative well-being extended to all, the essential goods were no longer scarce. Scarcity had in fact dominated the entire course of human evolution, and still dominates the life of the vast majority of humankind. In the past its rule had conditioned not only the economy, but also culture and customs. Accelerating the growth of human capital, and thus of productivity, the end of scarcity pointed in the direction of what is known as the post-industrial economy. In this economy industrial production is no longer prevalent—neither as output nor as income—while immaterial production gains ever more ground (albeit often advancing on material supports).

To govern the new trend the need was for a targeted project pursuing the model of a society of abundance. This has never been done. Most observers have failed to move on from the development models prevalent before the welfare state. And yet in 1968 Rosdolsky was already stressing that the productive potentialities were by then able to free people from the slavery of the assembly line and repetitive work.[14] Today development calls for a steady increase in immaterial labour and consumption.[15] Even traditional material production must rest on a series of immaterial work

[13] FAO and OWD, Food—Food per Person.

[14] Rosdolsky (1968: 427–428).

[15] For a similar approach, see Bell (1973, chs. 1–2) and Hodgson (1999, chs. 9–11).

activities if it is to be efficient. This is the case not only in rich societies, but also in the developing economies.

Past theory helps us to understand the nature of the new consumption patterns. Smith, Say and Ricardo, unlike Malthus, held human desires to be unlimited, and that therefore there were no limits to accumulation. On the other hand, Smith and Ricardo contemplated above all an indefinite increase in material comfort, while Say made explicit reference to immaterial goods.[16] Actually, if only material goods are taken into consideration the inevitable outcome is to foresee accumulation eventually ceasing to give way to a stationary state.

This was the line taken by, among others, J.S. Mill and Keynes, who described the stationary state as one of abundance in which needs are finally satisfied and production limited to replacing the goods consumed. Freed from pressure and tensions, people dedicate their time to refining their taste and enhancing their culture.[17] However, Patten and Wicksell realised that the stationary state could lead to the prevalence of rents, as indeed has happened, and as Piketty confirms.[18]

In reality, today growth of human capital and immaterial goods constitutes an increasingly important part of accumulation. To illustrate this concept, let us look back to Engel's law. In the nineteenth century Engel demonstrated that the percentage of income spent on food shrinks as the overall income grows. Pasinetti generalised this law, stating that as income increases the proportion spent on superior consumption also increases; this consumption is ever less material and increasingly enhances human capital.[19] Kindleberger, for his part, extended Engel's law to factors of production. In the preindustrial age, he observes, the predominant factor of production was land; in the industrial age it was physical capital, but in the post-industrial economy the dominant factor is human capital.[20]

In human capital the dichotomy between consumption and production is fuzzy. The same processes can be seen as both consumption and production. The dividing line between leisure time and working time is also blurred, throwing the traditional discipline of work into disarray. There is no longer much sense in fixed timetables and intensive rates of work with

[16] Smith (1776, ch. I.11, Part II: paragraph 7). Say (1803, ch. I, XV:92), 1828–1829, ch. VII.4). Ricardo (1821: chs. 21.5, 21.7).

[17] J.S. Mill (1848, ch. IV.6). Keynes (1930).

[18] Patten (1896, ch. IV). Wicksell (1901, ch. 1.III: 214–215). For Piketty see Sect. 6.2.

[19] Pasinetti (1981, above all ch. 4).

[20] Kindleberger (1990: 5–21).

productivity being increasingly dependent on cultural consumption and creativity. Even measuring production itself is no longer sufficient to assess productivity, which is increasingly dependent on the workers' social and relational context and is hard to pin down and quantify.

5.2 Saturation and Blockage of the Welfare State

5.2.1 *The Degenerated Aspects of the Welfare State*

In the second half of the 1970s investments began to slow down while unemployment grew to become a permanent feature of the economies (see Sects. 6.1 and 6.2). Since then the western economy has seen phases of weak and partial recovery (due above all to the globalisation of trade and growth of digital production) alternating with phases of stagnation or acute crisis (like the 10-year-long crisis that began in 2007).

The Human Development Index (the measurement devised by Mahbub ul Haq), which had risen by 10 points (from 0.35 to 0.45) between 1950 and 1970, increased by only seven points (from 0.45 to 0.52 to) between 1970 and 1990.[21] From 1969 to 2019 the average per capita GDP increase in the OECD (Organisation for Cooperation and Economic Development) countries fell from 3% to less than 1%.[22] The crisis of the welfare state has, then, persisted to the present day. As usual, it began with saturation of the market, but this time it was not due to low wages and insufficient demand. *It was not an underconsumption crisis*, as in the 1930s. In the 1970s purchasing power was not lacking, but it produced rent rather than profit. Let us see why.

In the first phase of the welfare state increased employment and rising real wages (including public services and state support for the weaker categories) had generated a corresponding increase in productivity and extension of the commodities market. Eventually, however, social expenditure in the interests of individuals and categories ran to excess, independently of the increase in productivity. There were two reasons for this: to begin with, automatic protection mechanisms had been created that continued running regardless of the effective needs of the beneficiaries. Secondly, there was a series of abuses by individuals and categories which benefited from services to which they had no right (but there was also, as

[21] OWD, Work and Life—Human Development Index.
[22] Worldbank data (see Valentini 2019).

Roncaglia explains, the liberalisation of movements of capital, which led to fiscal competition amongst the states and thus a waning of state capacity for social protection and spending).[23]

These two factors produced a partial degeneration of the welfare state. Some swathes of the working classes underwent nothing less than an anthropological transformation, in the space of a few years moving on from poverty and hyper-exploitation misery to being kept (often illegally) entirely or partially by the state. At the same time, some members of the middle classes were not averse to benefiting—again, often illegally—from the public support provided for the working class. The public debt began to grow and while social spending for certain categories soared expenditure on public services was steadily whittled down. On top of all this, tax evasion was not uncommon among the middle classes, the money saved being invested in public debt bonds.

The demand shown by these—middle and working—classes, accustomed as they were to semi-parasitic practices, was not innovative: it was not for new goods, but for more traditional goods. At the same time, the state was cutting down on public services—that great sector that could have refuelled development and growth of human capital. In fact, the politicians found it more advantageous to channel spending into the various categories of voters rather than public services. For their part, the enterprises followed the trends and continued to produce traditional goods until the market was saturated. Society split up into so many corporative sections that transformed the profits of the welfare state into rents.

And production continued to supply the same goods as before, with no significant variations. Households filled their homes with these goods which, in accordance with Gossen's law,[24] proved to be of ever less real utility. Instead of producing new goods that could satisfy the new needs generated by the welfare state (e.g. mass higher education, efficient public transport, development of research, tourism and cultural activities, measures for the environment, new approaches to town planning and so forth), the market imposed repetitive goods—more televisions, cars and clothes. The households bought—and continue to buy—these repetitive goods driven by the relentless stimulus of a combination of factors: advertising, fashion, discounts, true or alleged improvement in products and

[23] Roncaglia (2019, ch. 4.7: 307–308).

[24] According to Gossen's laws, the utility of a good, and thus its value is inversely proportional to the quantity of that good available.

planned obsolescence. In the long run, however, spending on repetitive goods declined, the market was saturated and crisis loomed up.

This degeneration of social policies, albeit only very partial, nevertheless led to discredit being brought on the whole welfare state. Baran and Sweezy went back to the old underconsumption idea that expenditure on welfare had been unproductive, serving only to avoid the excessive surplus that would have blocked accumulation.[25] The prejudice that public expenditure is unproductive (see Sect. 2.2.4) has meant serious harm for the welfare state.[26] According to the classical economists (including Marx), production of wealth can only be accomplished through the profit of the private enterprises. Public expenditure is subtracted from profit, and the lower it is, the better (see Sect. 2.2.2). Most of the neoclassicals (and some Marxists, too) shared this approach, despite some significant exceptions including Alvin Hansen and Kuznets.[27]

In 1966 William J. Baumol argued that public expenditure has a productivity of its own which grows more slowly than that of the private sector, but its wages are equal. Thus, the more the productivity of the private sector increases, the more expenditure for the public sector will prove an unproductive burden. The need, then, was to take funding and shift it to the private sector. Atkinson had no difficulty in confuting this thesis, observing that better levels of healthcare and education (i.e. an increase in public sector productivity) boosts the productivity of the private sector.[28] Obvious as it is, this simple fact escapes many.

This approach led to the failure to distinguish between repetitive goods and new goods that satisfied new needs, or between productive expenditure and expenditure dictated by corporative selfishness. All distinctions were swallowed up in unthinking criticism of consumerism, and public opinion began to distrust Keynesian policies.[29] This opened the way to the neoliberal reaction of the 1980s. Finally, it is worth noting that the crisis of the welfare state was structural, although the economists who had lost sight of this concept (see Sect. 3.4) mistook it for a passing, business cycle crisis, and thought that it was enough to wait for the upturn of the cycle to set in again. They are still waiting.

[25] Baran and Sweezy (1966, chs. 6 and 7).

[26] Morroni (2018, dialogue 4). Plehwe et al. (2019, chs. 8 and 9).

[27] Hansen (1941: 144–152). Kuznets (1966: 224–234).

[28] See Atkinson (2015: 121–123).

[29] An example of this is to be seen in Bacon and Eltis (1976: 77–91).

5.2.2 Neoliberalism: From the Tyranny of Profit to the Return of Rent

In the times of the welfare state, the returns on capital (profit, rent, interest) reached their peak, after which they began to decline.[30] Faced with the first signs of saturation, how did the enterprises react? Instead of pressing for a revival of development, they took advantage of the situation to break the social pact which had governed the boom. Towards the end of the 1960s, Western Europe had come close to that full employment pursued by the (post)-Keynesians, with consequent increase in the bargaining power of the employed. On top of this, there were some groups of workers that, egged on by the student movements, were flatly contesting capitalism as such. The entrepreneurs reacted with alarm.

The reaction of the enterprises was to take back control over accumulation. The big factories were split up into smaller units. Union rights came under attack, together with the "dependency culture" of the welfare state and state "interference" in the economy. At the political level, Greece, Chile and Argentina were shaken by coups d'état, Mexico and Italy by massacres organised with the complicity of some of the state forces. The 1980s were dominated by the slogan "more market, less state". Both the roles historically attributed to the state—creator/guarantor of rules and supplier of basic social services—were reduced to the minimum.

With the first of these roles the state lays down the rules for economic behaviour and sees that they are respected, guaranteeing—to some extent, at least—fair competition and distribution, rewarding merit. As Smith had warned with foresight, to guarantee competition the smaller and less privileged economic agents must be protected (see Sect. 2.1.2). With neoliberalism the state has seen these functions expropriated through deregulation.[31] In the neoliberal society it is the groups with corporative interests that dominate, tax evasion is made easy; in practice, taxation switches from progressive to regressive (the richer you are, the lower the percentage you pay) and extreme inequality becomes rife (see Sect. 6.2.2).

With the second of these roles the state provides the essential services (public administration, infrastructures, health, education, welfare and housing for the working classes) that keep the economy running. But neoliberalism has reduced such "unproductive" expenditure to the minimum,

[30] See Piketty (2014: 199–203) on the United Kingdom and France.

[31] Gallegati (2015: 29–30).

and the essential services have become inefficient and inadequate. This leads to unemployment and hits the weaker classes harder.

In 1993 Jacques Delors, president of the European Commission, proposed a courageous plan to reboot European development driven by public investments. The aim was to boost employment by investing in the new systems of infrastructure, information technology, biotechnologies and extending education.[32] The plan never got off the ground. Austerity and the chimera of a balanced budget prevailed.

The revolt that broke out in Chile in October 2019 exposed the failure of neoliberalism. In 1973 the Chilean *golpe*, backed by the American government, imposed the "Chicago boys" model in the most radical version that had not proved feasible even in the USA. For decades the macroeconomic data had created the impression that the Chilean economy was growing, but in reality it was only the wealth of the elite that grew, while society was impoverished. With the 2019 uprising the real data found their way to the media: the richest 1% holds 26.5% of the wealth; the richest 10% holds 60% of it. Everything has been privatised: water, electric power, transport, school and university education, healthcare and forestry. Consequently, the cost of living has soared while wages show no increase and treatment in the workplace is close to slavery.

Evans tellingly associates the 1970–1980 crisis with the Great Recession of 2008; according to the IMF (International Monetary Fund), between 1980 and 2010, 20 industrialised countries saw a 40% increase in the gap between the highest and lowest income deciles. This was due to the decline of the unions. In fact, after the oil shocks of the 1970s, collective contracts were taken to pieces in the UK and the USA, and Keynesian policies abandoned. The link between productivity and wages was broken. In the most industrialised and most unionised states of America antiunion laws called "right-to-work laws" were passed. The increasing inequality—which the ILO (International Labour Office) called "the crisis before the crisis"—led to the crash of 2008. But, incredible as it may seem, the inequalities continued to grow even after the crash.[33]

In the USA, from 1968 to 2013 the percentage of GDP going into wages dropped from 63.6 to 55.9. The percentage going to profits stood at 48 in 1950, dropped to less than 46 by 1974, but from then on went on rising up to nearly 54 by 2013. In the meantime taxation on enterprises

[32] Delors et al. (1993).
[33] Evans (2019).

fell from 4% to less than 2% of the GDP.[34] Piketty traces out a similar trend. Between 1950 and 1980 the share of national income of the richest decile in the USA fell to below 35%, to bounce back to 50% by 2008. In the UK, France and Germany, private wealth corresponded to 6–7 times the national annual income in the early years of the twentieth century; as from 1910 it declined, to reach 2–3 times in the period 1950–1970, but then picked up again. Piketty concludes that the returns on rent and shareholding tend to exceed the growth rate of the economy, with the exception of the period of the welfare state.[35]

To cope with saturation, new outlets for production were sought in the 1980s (see below). On one hand, investments went into technological progress, creating the great digital revolution that is still underway. On the other hand, globalisation was launched to boost exports. These two great processes have revolutionised production and consumption, but—due to state policies imbued with neoliberalism—instead of bolstering the economy of the developed countries they ended up by aggravating their crisis.

5.3 New Factors in Unemployment

5.3.1 *The Digital Revolution*

Ever since personal computers came into general circulation in the early 1980s, the digital revolution has shown no signs of slowing down; indeed, it continues spreading into new fields and creating unprecedented types of consumption goods. The use of software and algorithms is revolutionising all the sectors of production and distribution, even the most traditional and niche sectors. Thanks to digital processes labour productivity has increased far more than in any of the previous revolutions, and employment has shown a drastic decline.

However, the increase in productivity resulting from digital technologies shows an extremely uneven distribution amongst countries, sectors and enterprises. It finds little scope in unskilled material and labour but grows exponentially in the most advanced enterprises engaged in information technology, robotics, biotechnologies and mass distribution. Thus the increase in productivity and wealth appears ever more concentrated, leaving great masses of people impoverished. Between 2001 and 2013, 5%

[34] Apel (2015: 5 and 8).
[35] Piketty (2014: 23–27).

of the service enterprises saw productivity increase by 40%, while the remaining 95% of enterprises registered a mere 10% increase.[36]

The previous technological revolutions involved only certain sectors of production or commerce. None had revolutionised almost all the sectors of economic activity, as indeed is the case today. The previous revolutions may have created unemployment, but they boosted investments and eventually, with them, employment (see Sect. 3.4). Some authors argue that we are now on the same path, but it hardly seems likely. The present revolution is too widespread and the reduction in labour too radical for employment to bounce back to the previous level. In 1965, Gordon Moore, co-founder of Intel, stated that the number of transistors per microchip would double every 12 months (Moore's first law). Experience has borne out his forecast. Thus came what has been called the digital divide, namely a widening gap between those who have a grounding in the new information technologies (and in general in immaterial production) and those who have not.[37]

Moreover, the new international division of labour shaped by globalisation delegates to the emerging countries almost all the industrial production that not so long ago had had its fulcrum in the West. Consequently, western investment is concentrated in the sectors of the digital economy (information technology, robotics, 3D, biotechnologies, Big Data), entailing higher unemployment and reducing the percentage of staff in the more advanced enterprises by anywhere between 30% and 90%. Despite the drop in the last 2–3 years, unemployment still stands at 7.5% in the Eurozone.[38] And the upturn in employment registered in many developed countries should be viewed with due circumspection. It is largely based on insecure and occasional jobs, although it is in the interests of the governments to pass it off as normal increase in employment. As a result of persisting unemployment, the bargaining power of the workers is extremely weak. No end of precarious, overexploited positions have been created with few guarantees if any. The effects of the technological revolution make themselves felt mainly in the increasing inequality between jobs in terms of both quality and pay.

There is, however, a basic ambiguity in the development of new technologies. Ever more rapid innovation has brought the costs of information

[36] OECD data, in Kastrop and Ponattu (2018).
[37] See e.g. Haskel and Westlake (2018, ch. 6).
[38] Eurostat—Unemployment, July 2019.

technology services close to zero (which means that GDP, based on prices, is no longer a reliable measure of wealth).[39] This is to the advantage of consumers; indeed, Rifkin maintains that it is the beginning of the democratic economy led by the logic of the Commons.[40] In reality, the digital oligopolies offer free services to extend the range of their users, whose personal data—automatically recorded through the user's choices—are structured in the consumers' profiles. These profiles are sold to firms that can exploit them to target advertising to the customer's preferences.[41] Some authors argue that the "profiled" customers should demand payment of part of the value of the data collected;[42] or that the digital economy should be reformed to serve the public interest, seeing that the platforms they use were built with public money.[43]

Concealed data collection also extends to the workers employed by many firms and their behaviours.[44] For example, the Uber drivers have brought legal action against the company for accessing their personal data and their assessments of their work.[45] The sale of profiles is also carried out by semi-clandestine agencies which use them to influence voting behaviours (as came to light with the scandal of the British *Cambridge Analytica*). Shoshana Zuboff has published an impressive analysis of what she calls "surveillance capitalism". Zuboff holds that an intricate system has been created to survey the behaviour of every user of Internet, systematically violating their privacy.[46]

It is, of course, true that employment could start growing again if the appropriate investments were made in the new needs (see Sect. 8.3). But we have yet to see any encouraging signs of this. There is just the—still vague—project of the European Commission: the European Green Deal, launched on 11 December 2019, which provides for large-scale allocations (€260 billion a year for 10 years) aiming at carbon neutrality by 2050. We can only hope it will have better luck than Delors' project.

[39] Danovaro and Gallegati (2019: 101–102).
[40] Rifkin (2014: 287–289).
[41] Zuboff (2019, ch. 2–5).
[42] Arrieta Ibarra et al. (2017).
[43] Mazzucato (2019).
[44] Zuboff (2019, ch. 13).
[45] See Pettersson (2019).
[46] Zuboff (2019, ch. 6).

5.3.2 *Globalisation*

The other major outlet for the West lay in increased exports, incentivised by reducing customs duties. This policy, called globalisation, was decided upon by the governments of Europe at the end of the 1970s, partly in response to pressure exerted by the multinationals. Agreement on lower duties was reached through bilateral and multilateral treaties, or through WTO (World Trade Organization) policies. Terms of trade are usually imposed on the weaker countries, favouring the multinationals and their lobbies in the stronger countries.[47]

Globalisation was launched in the name of the ideology of free trade but with the tacit aim of coping with saturation. International trade was effectively enhanced, but the ultimate effects contradicted expectations. In international trade the Western countries were accustomed to imposing the prices that answered to their own interests, and believed that liberalisation would extend precisely the same mechanism they were used to. However, a new process came under way when some non-Western countries began to develop and loom larger in the international markets.

The liberalisation of trade catalysed development in the so-called Asian tigers (South Korea, Thailand, Taiwan and Singapore), then also in Mexico, Brazil, South Africa, Nigeria, India and, above all, China. To these are added the countries of Eastern Europe, developing rapidly under the protective umbrella of the EU. For the emerging countries, development is based above all on industrialisation, the engine being powered by exports. Between 1950 and 2000 the percentage of international trade accounting for world GDP rose from 8% to 27%.[48]

Thanks to the liberalisation of trade, these countries have to some extent shaken off their old subordinate roles (assembly, production of secondary components). Thanks to low wages, the emerging countries are now on the winning side in competition with the rich countries.[49] For the emerging countries, industrialisation is also being achieved on the strength of the investments and relocations of the Western enterprises in pursuit of low wages, tax exemptions and slacker control. But for the poorest countries globalisation has tightened the Western grip yet further, holding back their development (see Sect. 8.1).

[47] Baker (2016, ch. 7).
[48] Vaggi (2018: 132).
[49] Palley (2018: 18–31).

Such a ground-breaking transition should have advanced on more gradual, controlled lines. But the rich countries found it more convenient to go on exploiting the Third World through several policies, called as a whole neo-colonialism, and continue with their traditional production to the point of market saturation. They still lack strategies for post-industrial growth, without which deindustrialisation is becoming a deadly trap for the West.

References

Apel, Holger (2015) "Income Inequality in the U.S. from 1950 to 2010", *Real World Economics Review*, 72: 2–15.

Arrieta Ibarra, Imanol et al. (2017) "Should We Treat Data as Labor? Moving Beyond 'Free'", *American Economic Association Papers & Proceedings*, 1(1), online.

Atkinson, Anthony B. (2015) *Inequality*, Cambridge, MA and London: Harvard University Press.

Bacon, Robert and Eltis, Walter (1976) *Britain's Economic Problem: Too Few Producers*, London: Macmillan.

Bairoch, Paul (1997) *Storia economica e sociale del mondo*, trans. of *Victoires et déboires. Histoire économique et sociale du monde du XVIe siècle à nos jours*, Torino: Einaudi, 1999.

Baker, Dean (2016) *Rigged: How Globalization and the Rules of the Modern Economy were Structured to Make the Rich Richer*. Washington, DC: Center for Economic and Policy Research.

Baran, Paul and Sweezy, Paul (1966) *Monopoly Capitalism*. New York and London: Modern Reader, 1968, online

Bell, Daniel (1973) *The Coming of Post-industrial Society*, New York: Basic Books.

Danovaro, Roberto and Gallegati, Mauro (2019) *Condominio Terra*, Firenze and Milano: Giunti.

Delors, Jacques et al. (1993) *Crescita, competitività, occupazione … Libro bianco*, Bruxelles and Lussemburgo: Commissione delle Comunità Europee.

Evans, John (2019) "Inequality and Unions …", *Social Europe*, Jan. 23.

Gallegati, Mauro (2015) *The Economy of the Hamster*, World Economic Association, eBook.

Hansen, Alvin (1941) *Fiscal Policy and Business Cycle*, London: Allen & Unwin.

Haskel, Jonathan and Westlake, Stian (2018) *Capitalism without Capital*, Princeton and Oxford: Princeton University Press.

Hobson, John A. (1894) *The Evolution of Modern Capitalism*, online Internet Archive.

Hodgson, Geoffrey M. (1999) *Economics and Utopia*, New York and Abingdon: Routledge.
Kastrop, Christiand and Ponattu, Dominic (2018) "Why Weak Competition Can Increase Inequality in Europe", *Social Europe*, Dec. 18, 2018.
Kautsky, Karl (1902) *Teorie della crisi*, trans. from German, partially in L. Colletti and C. Napoleoni, eds., *Il futuro del capitalismo. Crollo o sviluppo?* Bari: Laterza, 1970: 271–296.
Keynes, John Maynard (1930) "Economic Possibilities for Our Grandchildren", in *Essays in Persuasion*, New York: Norton, 1963: 358–373, online yale.edu.
Kindleberger, Charles (1990) *Leggi economiche e storia dell'economia*, trans. from English, Roma and Bari: Laterza.
Kuznets, Simon (1966) *Modern Economic Growth*, New Haven, CT: Yale University Press.
Lindert, Peter (2016) *Real and Imagined Threats to the Welfare State*, online Working Paper, Oct. 11.
Loria, Achille (1889) *Analisi della proprietà capitalista*, 2 vols., in Id., *Opere*, vol 1, Torino: UTET, 1957: 1–656; vol. 2, Torino: Bocca, online: openbess from University of Torino.
Mazzucato, Mariana (2013) *Lo Stato innovatore* [*The Entrepreneurial State*], Roma and Bari: Laterza.
——— (2018) *The Value of Everything*, Allen Lane and Penguin.
——— (2019) "Preventing Digital Feudalism", *Social Europe*, Oct. 9.
Mill, John Stuart (1848) *Principles of Political Economy with Some of Their Applications to Social Philosophy*, 7th ed. London: Longmans & Green, 1909, online Library of Economics & Liberty.
Morroni, Mario (2018) *What Is the Truth about the Great Recession and Increasing Inequality?*, Springer.
OWD (*Our World in Data*), ed. by Max Roser, online https://ourworldindata.org/.
Palley, Thomas (2018) *Three Globalizations, Not Two*, FMM Working Paper, No. 18, online, Hans-Böckler-Stiftung.
Pasinetti, Luigi (1981) *Dinamica strutturale e sviluppo economico* [trans. of *Structural Change and Economic Growth*], Torino: UTET, 1984.
Patten, Simon (1896) *The Theory of Social Forces*, Philadelphia: American Academy of Political & Social Science, online Internet Archive.
Pettersson, Karin (2019) "Can Data-Labour Unions Break the Monopoly Capture of Data?", *Social Europe*, Apr. 1.
Piketty, Thomas (2014) *Capital in the Twenty-First Century*, Cambridge, MA and London: Harvard University Press, trans. from French ed. (2013) and updated.
Plehwe, Dieter et al. eds. (2019) *Austerity. 12 Myths Exposed*, Social Europe, online.
Ricardo, David (1821) *Principles of Political Economy and Taxation*, London: Murray, online Library of Economics & Liberty.

Rifkin, Jeremy (2014) *La società a costo marginale zero*, trans. from English, Milano: Mondadori, 2014.

Roncaglia, Alessandro (2019) *L'età della disgregazione. Storia del pensiero economico contemporaneo*, Bari and Roma: Laterza, ebook.

Rosdolsky, Roman (1968) *The Making of Marx's 'Capital'*, trans. from German and London: Pluto Press, 1977, online: gruppegrundrisse.files.wordpress.com.

Say, Jean-Baptiste (1803) *Traité d'économie politique*, 6th ed. Paris: Guillaumin, 1841, online Inst. Coppet.

——— (1828–1829) *Cours complet d'économie politique pratique*, 2nd ed. Paris: Guillaumin, 1840, 2 vols.

Smith, Adam (1776) *Wealth of Nations*, E. Cannan ed. London: Methuen, 1904, online Library of Economics & Liberty.

Tcherneva, Pvlina (2015) "Trends in US Income Inequality", *Real-World Economics Review*, 71: 64–74.

Vaggi, Gianni (2018) *Development*, Palgrave Macmillan Pivot.

Valentini, Ezio (2019) "Structural Crisis and Robotisation Require More Europe, Less Austerity", *Social Europe*, June 4.

Van Mol, Christof and de Valk, Helga (2016) "Migration and Immigrants in Europe …", in *Integration Processes and Policies in Europe*, B. Garcés-Mascareñas and R. Penninx, eds., Imiscoe and Springer, 31–55.

Wicksell, Knut (1901) *Lectures on Political Economy*, trans. from Swedish, vol. 1, Fairfield: Kelley, 1977; online Von Mises inst.

Zuboff, Shoshana (2019) *The Age of Surveillance Capitalism*, London: Profile Books.

CHAPTER 6

Broken Promises

Abstract When it was on the rise, capitalism promised jobs for all, efficient public services, reduction of inequalities within the limits of differences in merit, respect of civil, human and labour rights, and crackdown on abuses and illegality. Today, however, the data show widespread unemployment, increasingly insecure jobs involving exploitation, tax evasion on a very large scale, poorer public services, and a huge increase in inequalities. Society is divided between the protected and unprotected categories; the superrich are domineering, slavery finds ample room in full-fledged capitalistic systems and the illegal and criminal economy is thriving, inextricably intermingling with the legal economy.

Keywords Unemployment • Poverty • Inequalities • Capitalistic slavery • Illegal economy

Fred Hirsch (1976) came up with a telling analysis of the promises broken by a capitalism that guaranteed social and economic success to the individual. However, apart from the individual promises examined by Hirsch, there are also the social promises that have been broken—promises of great conquests for civilisation. It was thanks to these promises that capitalism had prevailed over the other economic systems: decent jobs available to all, general well-being, no excessive inequalities, no more arbitrary treatment or abuse, merit and interpersonal relations prevailing over

© The Author(s) 2020

C. Perrotta, *Is Capitalism Still Progressive?*,
https://doi.org/10.1007/978-3-030-48169-8_6

privilege and patronage. Today these great conquests are by no means certain. In the past, the dark side of capitalism had been limited to the colonised countries and most exploited classes (far from the eyes of the upper and middle classes), but now the shadow is spreading over all of Western society.

The period from 1980 to 2010 saw a great increase in private wealth, above all in Europe and Japan. Now growth is slower, but private savings are very high while public saving is negative. The share of public capital is steadily dwindling, and this is dragging on growth.[1] In 2010, Piketty points out, the capital/income ratio was 5:1 (more or less as it was on the eve of the First World War) and the trend is still rising (ibid.: 195–196). Thus we are back to a state of low growth, as in the Belle Époque. In this "patrimonial" capitalism, increasing importance is going to wealth accumulated in the past (ibid.: 232–233).

6.1 Unemployment

6.1.1 Unemployment, Insecure Jobs, Poverty

As we have seen, unemployment is increasing in the Western countries. In the Eurozone and Great Britain it has risen from roughly 2% in the period of the welfare state to the present 7–8%, but for the young it stands at 16%.[2] On top of this, in 2018 over 17% of Europeans aged between 25 and 35 were NEET: Not in Employment, Education or Training. We have also seen that three factors lie behind unemployment: market saturation and the consequent drop in investment, the technological revolution cutting jobs, and the relocation of industries to the emerging countries.

However, we shouldn't lose sight of a fourth factor, illustrated by Loretta Napoleoni: the collapse of the Soviet Union and the communist regimes. It has thrown onto the labour market millions of unemployed who, besides adding to the criminal economy and sexual slavery, have lowered the level of wages and protection of workers.[3] Increasing

[1] Piketty (2014: 183–187).

[2] Eurostat—Unemployment. Atkinson (2015: 133–134).

[3] Napoleoni (2008, chs. 1 and 2).

unemployment is progressively eroding working conditions, beginning with the level of wages. Today the newly hired workers are on contracts with far lower pay and levels of protection than were enjoyed by workers taken on in the past decades. This entails the systematic destruction of human capital.

As a result of technical progress and the concentration of capital, labour tends to be polarised.[4] For example, the growing consumption of energy is leading to capital-saving innovations which generate networks run by experts. These networks cover a highly varied range, from electricity to traffic control, research, agriculture and health services. Another example is to be seen in the great digital enterprises that absorb the small ones, concentrating profits thanks to the collection of Big Data and ownership of the algorithms regulating them (Sect. 5.2.2).

Precarious working conditions arise from fixed-term employment contracts, fake self-employment (exempting the employer from tax and social security contributions), and lack of paid holidays, free medical assistance and provision for pensions. Involuntary part-time work accounts for a large share of the insecure jobs. According to the European Commission, in 2012 between 10% and 18% of part-time jobs in central Europe were involuntary, but the percentage rose to over 50% in southern Europe.[5]

The welfare state had reduced poverty very considerably, but now it is increasing again. Today the "vicious circle of poverty" described by the development economists of the 1950s still prevails in the backward countries.[6] The negative economic factors (low demand on the market, low productivity and poor qualifications for work, lack of capital, low income, hidden unemployment, etc.) coalesce and choke growth. Today, in the West poverty is increasing in a dynamic context as a result, rather, of a cumulative process, like the one described by Myrdal: the factors act upon one another aggravating the negative trends and leading the economy towards collapse.[7] For example, increasing unemployment means decreasing demand on the market, which discourages investment, and this in turn drives up unemployment yet further.

[4] See Ernst (2019).
[5] Atkinson (2015: 136, 138).
[6] See e.g. Nurkse (1951: 7). Meier and Baldwin (1957: 319–324).
[7] Myrdal (1957: 20).

6.1.2 Fiscal Crisis and Decline of Public Services

James O'Connor wrote that in capitalist societies, the competitive sector shows a marked resistance to paying taxes, and tax avoidance and evasion are rife. This resistance is due not only to the low profit margins in the sector, but above all because the taxes go to the advantage of the monopolistic sector and the "unproductive" sector of the economy. Tax evasion leads to fiscal crisis for the state.[8] O'Connor's analysis still applies today. As we have seen (Sect. 5.2.2), the greatest tax evasion is accounted for by the oligopolistic multinationals (O'Connor's "monopolies"), especially in the digital area.

In absolute terms, there has been no fall in social spending in the developed countries,[9] but the quality of education, health services, housing policies and pension systems is deteriorating. The increased demand for quality for administration and infrastructures is not met. So much the better for the private enterprises, which often provide the same services on payment thanks to state facilitation and financing. This is one of the major factors generating inequality and increasing poverty.

The fiscal crisis faced by the state is also weighing on the professional framework of the various institutions. There has been a drastic reduction in the number of civil servants, whose average age is progressively rising. This process has not only lowered the quality of the services, but also weakens the mechanism for transmitting specialist skills to the new staff. Above all in the weaker capitalist economies, most of the present civil servants who retire are not being replaced. Piketty points out that at the end of the nineteenth century the revenue of the Western states stood at around 10% of the national income. Today, after the welfare state and increased social spending, it ranges between 30% (USA) and 55% (Sweden), while in the poorer countries it comes to 10–15%. The need, then, is to increase taxation on the higher incomes, fight evasion and control the movement of capital.[10]

[8] O'Connor (1973).
[9] OWD—Government Spending.
[10] Piketty (2014: 471–535).

6.2 Inequalities

Capitalism had promised to reduce inequalities, accepting only those generated by merit. Today, however, inequalities are increasing in the West, and are far worse than those brought about by the crisis of the 1930s, which in fact saw a fall in the income of the richest 10%. By contrast today it is rising out of all proportion.

6.2.1 *The Transformation of Capital into Rents (on Finance and Real Estate)*

The transformation of capital into rents is one of the major causes of the increase in inequalities, and is in fact the trend that appears most to contradict the rationale of capitalism. With the welfare state, wages and profits grew together while rents were on the decline. Fifty years later, the picture is quite the reverse: the wages and incomes of the unprotected classes have plunged while profits are growing but rents are growing even more.[11]

Atkinson recalls the powerful appeal, noted by John Kenneth Galbraith, of competition in the capitalistic market. It ensured that economic power was diffuse and not under the arbitrary control of anyone.[12] Alas, this is ever less the case. The trend towards concentration has led to the domination of a few oligopolies, which distort competition in their own favour and tend to transform profits into rents—a trend described by Berle and Means in the 1930s, and subsequently by Schumpeter (1942). Piketty points out that the states of Europe had never been so rich as they are today, but this wealth is distributed very unevenly. "Private wealth rests on public poverty", and so "we currently spend far more in interest on the debt than we invest in higher education".[13]

Today financial speculation is the main source of income,[14] and it is also the main cause of inequality.[15] Financial speculation has always existed in capitalism, because the big enterprises obtain their financing through

[11] See Franzini and Pianta (2016, 2.3: 95–106).

[12] Atkinson (2015: 123–127).

[13] Piketty (2014: 567).

[14] Bichler and Nitzan (2015) acutely criticise the incapacity of theory to distinguish between real production and the financial economy. However, the examples they give risk confusing two very different things, namely financial speculation and the immaterial production of wealth.

[15] See Corm (1993: 27–31). James Galbraith (2019), Gallino (2013: 62–70).

loans from the small savers, selling bonds to them. With trade in bonds on the stock exchange a certain degree of financial speculation inevitably develops as a side-effect. However, when it spreads too far it can cause sudden slumps of all the bonds. In the nineteenth century a number of authors had warned that a disproportionate increase in the financial sector creates "fictitious capital", subject to collapse.[16] From the 1980s on, saturation has shifted a great deal of capital towards financial speculation, which has grown abnormally.

In 1980 the world GDP in production of non-financial goods and services stood at around 27,000 billion dollars, and the financial assets came to more or less the same amount. But in 2007 financial gains proved four times greater than the GDP of real production: 240 thousand billion as against 60 thousand. In 2013 financial transactions came to at least 50 times more than the overall trade in goods and services.[17] Today, the total of private and public debts corresponds to 320% of the world income.[18]

With information technology there are no limits in space or time to the operations on the stock exchange, and this has facilitated manipulation of the data. Everywhere, finance has seen frenzied expansion. A vast range of derivatives has burgeoned. Brought in as a form of insurance against the risks of financial transactions, derivatives have proved to be quite the opposite—sheer gambling, fraught with risks. Deceptive bonds have been created with incomprehensible calculation of returns, eliciting the confidence of savers.[19] The banks sold these bonds to productive enterprises, convincing them that they should "diversify their portfolio";[20] and to public administrations, having them pay very low interest at the outset, only to burden the future administrators with usurious interest rates.

This economic decline has become moral decline. The banks have issued trash bonds, hoodwinking their own clients, or channelled the clients' savings into risky speculation or to finance other speculators. Often the state has had to step in to save them from failure, to avoid creating panic. All this has left in its wake a keen sense of resentment and diffidence which is fraying the social fabric. Savers have now become afraid of

[16] See e.g. Marx (1863–83), *Capital III*, ch. 25.
[17] Gallino (2013, ch. 1 and p. 35).
[18] Biasco (2019, section 3).
[19] See Napoleoni (2008: 57–63).
[20] On the "financialization" of enterprises, see Salento and Masino (2013, ch. 5).

investing in stocks and shares and are falling back on the purchase of real estate or gold.

On top of financial speculation has come speculation in real estate. Speculation in buildable land, housing and buildings has been used as a remedy for saturation. The US real estate crisis which triggered the world-wide crash of 2008 was brought on by the pursuit of easy gains.

As Michael Hudson writes: "The Federal Reserve's QE3 [i.e. the third Quantitative Easing operation] has flooded the stock and bond markets with low-interest liquidity. This makes it profitable for speculators to borrow cheap and make arbitrage gains buying stocks and bonds yielding higher dividends or interest (…) In the Bubble Economy, families became convinced that the way to build up their wealth was to borrow as much as they could to buy the most expensive home they could, and ride the wave of asset-price inflation. But since 2008, consumers have paid down about $5 trillion of personal debt".[21]

Real estate speculation is accompanied by exorbitant rents strangling small and large shops, restaurants, and so on, often accounting for two thirds of the management's takings. And recently a new form of speculation has emerged—land grabbing. Overpopulated states like China and exporters of agricultural produce like the USA, as well as desert states seeking cultivable land, like Saudi Arabia and Qatar,[22] are buying vast swathes of land from the poorest state through the multinationals or with the capital of financial speculation.[23] Such is the case in particular with Africa, Brazil and the rest of Latin America, Southeast Asia and Eastern Europe.[24] The land is usually sold or rented out with century-long contracts unbeknownst to the inhabitants who, to survive, have no choice but to abandon their land.

A more traditional way of grabbing land is associated with the construction of huge dams for the production of electric power or setting to work on mines and oil wells. The Chinese dams on the Yellow River and the Aswan Dam on the Nile had destructive effect, submerging entire villages and cultivated land that hundred thousands of people lived on. A similar case has recently occurred in the Omo Valley in Ethiopia.[25]

[21] Hudson M. (2015: 59–60).
[22] Liberti (2011, ch. 2).
[23] Ibid., chs. 3 and 4.
[24] See the detailed analysis of this phenomenon in Grillotti and De Felice (2019).
[25] See Franchi G. and Manes (2016).

6.2.2 *Plutocracy and Growing Inequalities*

In the 1980s the "revolution of the rich"—as it was called—began with the proclamation that profit was actually a moral value as the fruit of merit. But then it went further, asserting that wealth in itself was a virtue. This was the basis for the theorisation of plutocracy and justification of all kinds of financial hoodwinking.[26]

In the twenty-year period 1970–1990, according to Piketty, in the Western countries the richest 10% of the population received about 25% of the total income, but in 2010 it was receiving 35% in Europe and 50% in the USA. As for the possession of wealth, in 2010 the richest 10% in Great Britain, France, Germany and Italy owned about 60% of it, and in the USA 72%. Note that these figures are underestimated because they are based on the statements of the interested parties. In the first decade of the twenty-first century, 1% of the population, owned half the world's wealth, and 0.1% owned about 20% of it.[27]

Many authors confirm the increase in inequality favouring the wealthiest as from 1980.[28] Baker has shown that the percentage of national income going to the richest 1%, *without counting capital gains*, had risen from 7.7% in 1973 to 18.3% by 2007, and did not drop from the level even after the crisis.[29] Cook (2018) stresses that inequality remained a neglected issue in economics throughout the twentieth century, largely because of the fundamental concepts of neoclassical theory including the theorem of "Pareto optimality" (see Sect. 8.3.1). This way of diverting attention has hardly helped to reduce inequalities. Stiglitz (2013) provides a clear explanation of the connection between growing inequalities and difficulties in development.

The Oxfam data for 2018 complete this dismal picture. In the world, just one year sufficed for the private wealth of 1900 billionaires to increase by $900 billion, while the wealth of the poorer half of the population (3.8 billion people) fell by 11%. The wealth held by this poorer half is *equal* to that of the 26 richest people in the world (but 43 in 2017). In 2018 Jeff Bezos, the founder of Amazon, declared a personal income of $112 billion. The wealth possessed by men is 50% higher than the wealth held by women, whose earnings fall short by 23%. It has been estimated that the

[26] See Franzini and Pianta (2016, 1.1 e 1.2: 17–24).
[27] Piketty (2014: 249, 257–258, 435–439).
[28] Atkinson (2015: 68–81). Ruccio and Morgan (2018: 16). See also Arlacchi (2018: 138).
[29] Baker (2016: 26–27).

unpaid housework and care work done by women is worth 10,000 billion dollars a year.[30]

The USA is the paradise of plutocracy. Alongside the slowdown in growth, as from 1980, inequalities have increased in favour of the richer white population. A series of laws fostered this trend, above all with financial deregulation.[31] Thus there has been a transfer of income from 1980 to the present day of no fewer than 15 points from the poorer 90% to the richer 10%. In the period 1987–2013 the biggest estates in the world grew about twice as much as all the others. These extreme inequalities, as Piketty points out, contributed to the economic crisis of 2007.[32]

The concentration of wealth is also to be seen in the case of enterprises. In 2017, 147 multinationals—accounting for far less than 1% of the total of enterprises—controlled 40% of the world's wealth.[33] The IMF (International Monetary Fund) has been indirectly helping along this process, inflicting usurious interest rates on the countries to which it lends funds, with ruinous consequences for the local enterprises.[34]

With the managers of the enterprises we come to another chapter in the story of robbing the weakest. They do not defend the interests of the firm because they only look to the short period results—the results that matter to the shareholders.[35] Their share in bonds issued by the firms has grown abnormally, so some rig the balance sheets to show non-existent profits.[36] In 1970 the pay of managers in the USA was on average 30 times higher than the average pay of the employees, but by 2016 it had grown to 271 times higher.[37]

This burgeoning of inequalities is due not only to antiunion laws and deregulation, but also to regressive fiscal laws. Leonhardt (2019) has recalled the famous complaint made ten years ago by the billionaire Warren Buffet, who found it absurd that he should pay lower taxes than his secretary. At the time the experts claimed that this was not the general trend, but it certainly is now. Today the richest 400 Americans pay lower taxes in percentage than all the other categories of taxpayers. In 1950 the richest

[30] Oxfam (2019: 5–14). For further relevant data, see *Credit Suisse* (2019).
[31] Williams (2017, ch. 9). Gallino (2013: 61 and ch. 3).
[32] Piketty (2014: 297–298).
[33] *Sustainable Equality* (2018: 68).
[34] Stiglitz (2001: IX).
[35] See Mazzucato and Jacobs (2016, ch. IV). Roncaglia (2019: 1157).
[36] Baker (2016, ch. 6).
[37] Ruccio and Morgan (2018: 22) from the Economic Policy Inst.

paid 70% of their income in taxes; by 1980 this had dropped to 47%, and today stands at 23%, while the poorer 50% pay about 24% of their income in taxes. According to Oxfam, in Brazil the richest 10% pay taxes (on their personal income + VAT) amounting to 21%, while the poorest 10% pay 32%. The UK shows a fairly similar situation (34% for the richest, 49% for the poorest).[38] It is hardly surprising that today 142 million Europeans are at risk of poverty (Dauderstädt 2019). And Buffet's complaint has been echoed by Bill Gates (reported in the media, 7 January 2020).

Over the last 40 years the taxes paid by the rich have been cut on the basis of the theorem that this reduces unproductive state expenditure and boosts investments thanks to the trickle-down effect.[39] The idea is that enrichment of those who are already rich benefits everyone because it translates into investments that increase the social wealth. Experience has shown how groundless this argument is. Regressive taxation has only impoverished the major part of society and clogged the tax havens with idle capital. Even the IMF itself argues (2018) that it is precisely the failure to redistribute resources that damages the economy. Today, at the world-wide level, property taxes account for only 4% of the total taxation.[40]

As was inevitable, the reduction of taxes for the rich has favoured tax avoidance and evasion on their part. For example, the digital oligopolies have wrested from the state tax exemption for almost all their assets (given that their services involve very high percentages of the population, the states are afraid they may be suspended). In 2004 the US multinationals paid taxes of 2.3% on their profits, which amounted to $700 billion.[41] According to the IMF, the states lose nearly $500 billion a year due to tax avoidance.[42] But blatant tax evasion is no less. According to Zucman, 40% of the foreign profits of the US multinationals is channelled into the tax havens. The great estates ending up in the tax havens exceed by far the foreign debts of the rich countries, accounting for about $7600 billion.[43]

The increasing inequalities registered in recent years apply not only to the richest as against the others, but are also to be seen in the rest of society.[44] When the welfare state took the downward path, new strata of needy

[38] Oxfam (2019: 23).
[39] See Vaggi (2018, *passim*: see Index).
[40] Oxfam (2019: 11–13 and 24).
[41] Gallino (2013: 62).
[42] See Stiglitz (2019). See also Stiglitz (2013).
[43] Zucman (2013: 47–55; chs. 3 and 5).
[44] See Franzini and Pianta (2016, 1.2: 25–28).

categories formed, and a twofold division came about: one between the protected middle classes (in general owners of real estate) and the unprotected classes, and another between the (not poor) elderly and the young. The protected part of the population consists of professionals and private employees with medium-to-high qualifications, persons with guaranteed incomes (in the public sector) and categories with strong union support. The non-protected have insecure or badly paid jobs, or meagre pensions, or are self-employed or mini-entrepreneurs in the weak categories. These categories feel that they have been cheated out of the security they once enjoyed.

The other division sees, on the one hand, elderly people with pensions or incomes ensuring security and a degree of well-being, and on the other hand young people and families with medium-to-low incomes. These young people have no choice but to chase after jobs with increasingly high qualifications (through study, specialisation or training), or alternatively resign themselves to doing badly paid jobs, often far below their qualifications. They face difficulties in accessing training for high specialisation or acquiring experience abroad. Thus the gap between guaranteed society and insecure society is widened.

6.3 Capitalistic Slavery Today

Capitalism had promised freedom in the choice of work and dignity for all workers, but slave labour is increasing. According to the historians, the ancient economies of Greece and Rome failed to generate capitalism above all because they were based on slavery, slave labour costing less than waged employment.[45] By definition, the slave economy offers no incentive to invest in and increase productivity, but capitalism has succeeded in reconciling slavery and profit perfectly well.

We have already considered some modern-day cases of capitalistic slavery in the Americas and Africa (see also Sects. 3.2.1, 4.1 and 4.2). In these cases production was for export, and depended on the demand of European countries. The exploitation of slaves was extreme, while the societies using them had poor, stagnant economies with parasitic elites. But in general, even when it depends on the multinationals, slavery holds back transition to a more modern and efficacious form of capitalistic accumulation.

[45] See Weber (1896) and Finley (1980).

Today capitalistic slavery has been reproduced thanks to the multinationals. In Pakistan, Bangladesh, Thailand, Burma, and so on, but also in the countries of central Africa, millions of children of poor families are sold to "entrepreneur" slave drivers who make them work for 14 hours a day, bound to the looms and punished for every irregularity. This is also the story of Iqbal Masih, the child who rebelled against slavery in Pakistan to become a trade unionist fighting it, and was eventually killed by the "carpet mafia" at the age of 12 in 1995. Apparently 94% of the work directly or indirectly used by the multinationals is of this type. *Freedom United*, *Walk Free* and various other online journals provide detailed documentation of modern-day slavery in the world.[46] The latest world economic crisis has boosted slave labour to save on the cost of labour.

The *Global Slavery Index 2018* (online) estimates that there are 40.3 million slaves in the world. Of these, 15 million are victims of forced marriages and about 25 million are set to forced labour. Women account for 71% of the slaves. For every thousand inhabitants of the world, 5.4 are slaves (rising to 7.6 in Africa). In the Arab states the figure is 3.3 per thousand, but the governments obstruct data collection and the figure is underestimated by far, for both forced marriages and forced labour. However, slavery is also present in the European countries.

For forced marriages Africa is the continent that is worst off, with 4.8 per thousand, while for forced labour it is Asia plus the Pacific area (with 4 per thousand), followed by Europe and Central Asia (in practice, the countries of the former USSR) with 3.6. The two countries with the worst records for slavery are ferocious dictatorships, North Korea and Eritrea, where about 10% of the inhabitants are reduced to slavery. Countries at war also show a high incidence of slavery. In India the slaves number nearly 8 million (about 6 per thousand) and in China nearly 4 million (2.8 per thousand). In the Eurasian area the worst countries are Turkmenistan and Byelorussia, at about 11 per thousand. But for Greece the figure stands at 8, for Russia 5.5, for Italy 2.5 and for Sweden 1.6.[47] In southern Europe semi-slavery is widespread (above all for immigrants) in the harvesting of fruit, stock farming, unskilled work in industry and the catering services. In Italy alone—according to Franchi (2019)—there are at least 200,000.[48]

[46] See also the documentation by Pozzi (2016, chs. 1 and 2).

[47] *Global Slavery Index*, *Regional Findings*, online.

[48] For the agriculture of Southern Italy, see Leogrande (2008).

According to the same source,[49] 152 million children are working in inhuman conditions. And in 2016 over 15,000 children were being used as child soldiers: 4000 in government armies and 11,500 in private armies. The number of child soldiers is increasing in Africa, but they are also to be found in Asia and Latin America. The countries with the highest proportions of slaves are, in decreasing order: North Korea, Eritrea, Burundi, the Central African Republic, Afghanistan, Mauritania, South Sudan, Pakistan, Cambodia and Iran. The governments making the least efforts to reduce slavery are in Qatar, Singapore, Saudi Arabia and the Emirates. In these countries slavery is reserved for the immigrant workers; their passports are taken away from them, and they are arrested if they try to escape.

An exemplary case of the slavery mechanism involves coltan, the precious mineral used in high-tech and aerospace industries, and so on. Mincone (2019) traces out the economic itinerary. To begin with, there is the labour of the child slaves in the Congo, the major producer; they earn two euros *a week*, and are exposed to radiation from the mineral and landslides. They are supervised by the child soldiers of the militia, the only authority in charge of the mining. Coltan is sold illegally to Belgian monopolistic companies, and from there passes on to other monopolistic companies in Germany, China and the USA for refinement. From here it moves on to the assembly firms in China and Southeast Asia, to end up in the products of the big firms (IBM, Toshiba, Siemens, etc.). It is worth noting that the "peace" mission that the USA is channelling most money into is in the Congo, to the benefit of the multinationals.

Finally, the World Health Organization estimates that about 10% of the over 126 thousand transplants performed in the world are illegal (in practice, a matter of organ trafficking). This foul commerce is worth between 840 and 1700 million dollars.[50]

6.4 The Illegal Economy is Expanding

Capitalism had promised legality and impersonal regulations, but the criminal economy is progressively spreading. The crisis facing the developed countries is at the same time economic and a crisis of values, and this encourages the growth of the illegal economy.[51] The growth has now

[49] *Global Slavery Index, Global Findings*: 28–29.
[50] For more detailed data on slavery, see *Walk Free* (2019).
[51] See Napoleoni (2008).

reached abnormal proportions, restricting the range of action of the legal economy and consensus in social values, challenging the idea that growth of profit depends on merit (entrepreneurship, industriousness, etc.). It is eroding the ultimate claim for superiority that capitalism has over the other economic systems. The illegal economy covers a vast range of mass behaviours including tax evasion, trade in counterfeit brands, illegal pollution produced by enterprises and individuals, corruption of public officials, illegal price cartels, tax havens, and so forth.

Outside the Western world, the illegal economy—including agriculture—reaches proportions of 50–60%.[52] As for Europe, the shadow economy appears to account for 19% of the GDP.[53] In Germany 18% of the financial capital (amounting to €331 billion) goes to the tax havens. In 2018, in online sale alone, counterfeit brands cost the luxury product firms about $30.3 billion.[54] The market for counterfeit articles of clothing, cosmetics and watches amounted to $450 billion.[55] Products displaying counterfeit trademarks are to be found in a vast range of sectors, including luxury cars.

Besides all this, there is the economy of organised crime, which is running the most thriving trade in the world, namely drugs,[56] as well as controlling the illegal arms traffic, prostitution rackets, all sorts of illegal gambling, trafficking in migrants and human organs, smuggling and money laundering, to name but a few of the activities. Walker (1999) conjectures that money laundering reaches a figure of $2.85 billion a year, concentrated mainly in Europe and North America. The various mafias also force their way into sharing ownership of healthy firms, among various other practices that often make it impossible to distinguish between the legal and illegal economy.

But there are also forms of illegality promoted or tolerated by certain states. One example is the tax havens, however they may be camouflaged. Then there is triangulation in arms trafficking, corruption of governments in countries producing oil or key minerals, destabilisation of governments that reject illegal agreements, land grabbing, financing local wars to control certain sources of wealth, and so forth. According to Gallino, the

[52] Madi (2015).
[53] Wikipedia, "Tax evasion".
[54] *Global Brand Counterfeiting Report* (vox.com).
[55] *The Fashion Law*, "The Counterfeit Report", October 11, 2018, online.
[56] UN *World Drug Report 2018*, book 1.

European political-economic establishment has contrived a rationale and practices that favour the illegal use of financial liberalisation.[57]

The activities of lobbies often condition political and administrative decisions, not always through direct corruption, but often by conditioning the environments. Between the influence of the lobbies and the legitimate pressure of voters there is a constant asymmetry of information to the detriment of the citizens. Akerlof explains how the asymmetry of information among private concerns can lead to fraud. But in the information asymmetry between certain private interests and the public interest it is the latter that in any case risks being harmed. Thus capitalism risks abandoning that progressive outlook that had favoured harmonisation of public and private interests and led to democracy.

References

Arlacchi, Pino (2018) *I padroni della finanza mondiale*, Milano: Chiare lettere.

Atkinson, Anthony B. (2015) *Inequality*, Cambridge, MA and London: Harvard University Press.

Baker, Dean (2016) *Rigged: How Globalization and the Rules of the Modern Economy Were Structured to Make the Rich Richer*, Washington, DC: Center for Economic and Policy Research.

Biasco, Salvatore (2019) "Il futuro dell'ordine mondiale neo-liberista …", *Il Mulino*, Feb.

Bichler, Shimshon and Nitzan, Jonathan (2015) "Capital Accumulation: Fiction and Reality", *Real-World Economics Review*, 72: 47–68.

Cook, Eli (2018) "The Great Marginalization: Why Twentieth Century Economists Neglected Inequality", *Real-World Economics Review*, 83: 20–34.

Corm, Georges (1993) *Il nuovo disordine economico mondiale*, trans. from French, Torino: Bollati Boringhieri, 1994.

Credit Suisse (2019) *Global Wealth Report*, online.

Dauderstädt, Michael (2019) "Tackling poverty and inequality in Europe", *Social Europe*, 15th Jan. 2019.

Ernst, Ekkehard (2019) "Big Data and Its Enclosure of the Commons", *Social Europe*, June 12.

Finley, Moses (1980) *Schiavitù antica e ideologie moderne*, trans. from English, Roma and Bari: Laterza, 1981.

Franchi, Massimo (2019) "Il neo-schiavismo nelle campagne. Intervista a Francesco Carchedi", *Diritti globali*, febbraio 18.

[57] Gallino (2013, ch. 5).

Franchi, Giulia and Manes, Luca (2016) *Che cosa c'è da nascondere nella Valle dell'Omo*, Re:Common, ebook.
Franzini, Maurizio and Pianta, Mario (2016) *Disuguaglianze*, Roma and Bari: Laterza, ebook.
Galbraith, James (2019) "A Global Macroeconomics ... of Inequality and Income Distribution", *Review of Keynesian Economics*, Spring 2019: 1–5.
Gallino, Luciano (2013) *Il colpo di stato di banche e governi*, Torino: Einaudi.
Grillotti, M. Gemma and De Felice, Pierluigi, eds. (2019) *I predatori della terra*, 2nd ed. Milano: Franco Angeli.
Hirsch, Fred (1976) *Social Limits to Growth*, London: Routledge, 1978.
Hudson, Michael (2015) *Finance as Warfare*, World Economic Association, e-book.
Leogrande, Alessandro (2008) *Uomini e caporali*, Milano: Mondadori.
Leonhardt, David (2019) "The Rich Really Do Pay Lower Taxes Than You", New York Times, Oct. 6, 2019.
Liberti, Stefano (2011) *Land Grabbing*, Roma: Minimum Fax.
Madi, Maria Alejandra (2015) "What is the Informal Economy?", WEA (World Economic Association) *Pedagogy Blog*, Aug. 8, 2015.
Marx, Karl, *Capital III* [1863–83], trans. from German, first ed. 1894, New York: International Publishers, online: marxists.org, 1999.
Mazzucato, Mariana and Jacobs, Michael, eds. (2016) *Ripensare il capitalismo*, trans. from English, Roma and Bari: Laterza.
Meier, G.M. and Baldwin, R.E. (1957) *Economic Development: Theory, History, Policy*, New York: Wiley.
Mincone, Alessandra (2019) "Congo. L'oro nero non è un gioco per i bambini minatori", *NENA (Near East News Agency) News*, Mar. 1.
Myrdal, Gunnar (1957) *Teoria economica e paesi sottosviluppati*, trans. from English, Milano: Feltrinelli, 1966.
Napoleoni, Loretta (2008) *Economia canaglia* (*Rogue Economics*), Milano: il Saggiatore, 2008.
Nurkse, Ragnar (1951) *La formazione del capitale nei paesi sottosviluppati*, trans. from English, Torino: Einaudi, 1965.
O'Connor, James (1973) *La crisi fiscale dello stato*, trans. from English, Torino: Einaudi, 1979.
OWD (*Our World in Data*), ed. by Max Roser, online https://ourworldindata.org/.
Oxfam (2019) "Oxfam Briefing Paper", Jan. 2019, Italian version, online: www.oxfam.it.
Piketty, Thomas (2014) *Capital in the Twenty-First Century*, Cambridge, MA and London: Harvard University Press, trans. from French ed. (2013) and updated.
Pozzi, Anna (2016) *Mercanti di schiavi*, Cinisello Balsamo (Milano): Ed. San Paolo.

Roncaglia, Alessandro (2019) *L'età della disgregazione. Storia del pensiero economico contemporaneo*, Bari and Roma: Laterza, ebook.

Ruccio, David and Morgan, Jamie (2018) "Capital and Class: Inequality after the Crash", *Real-World Economics Review*, 85: 15–24.

Salento, Angelo and Masino, Giovanni (2013) *La fabbrica della crisi*, Roma: Carocci.

Schumpeter, Joseph A. (1942) *Capitalismo, socialismo, democrazia*, trans. from English, Milano: Comunità, 1964.

Stiglitz, Joseph (2001) Foreword to Polanyi (1944) *The Great Transformation*, Boston: Beacon, 2001.

——— (2013) *The Price of Inequality*, New York and London: Norton.

——— (2019) "Corporate Tax Avoidance: It's No Longer Enough to Take Half Measures", *The Guardian*, International ed., Oct. 7, 2019, online.

Sustainable Equality (2018) Report of the EU Independent Commission for Sustainable Equality, online.

Vaggi, Gianni (2018) *Development*, Palgrave Macmillan, Pivot.

Walk Free (2019) *Measurement, Action, Freedom* (*Eradicate Modern Slavery*), Minderoo Foundation, online.

Walker, John (1999) How Big is Global Money Laundering? *Journal of Money Laundering Control* 3 (1): 25–37.

Weber, Max (1896) "Le cause sociali del tramonto della civiltà antica", in Id., *Storia economica e sociale dell'antichità*, trans. from German, Roma: Editori Riuniti, 1981.

Williams, Robert B. (2017) *The Privileges of Wealth*, London and New York: Routledge.

Zucman, Gabriel (2013) *The Hidden Wealth of Nations*, Chicago and London: University of Chicago Press, 2015, trans. from French.

CHAPTER 7

The New Challenges

Abstract Today we are witnessing the dire consequences of new crisis factors. Industrialisation, the greatest conquest of capitalism, is ruining the environment through both production and consumption, as attested by the data on the poisoning of the air, water and soil, plastic encroaching on every corner of the earth and seas. This also applies to global warming, despite the negationist campaigns backed by oil tycoons. Finally, emigration to the rich countries—due to demographic, economic and cultural factors—is causing in the West a serious crisis in social cohesion, threatening the stability of states. However, tackled with courage these factors can get development moving again through the post-industrial economy and growth of human capital.

Keywords Industrialisation • Environment destruction • Global warming • Emigration • Social cohesion

Over the last thirty years further circumstances have arisen that are jeopardising development. They show that the economy of profit, as it is structured today, cannot produce overall development since it leads to negation of both general growth and the very values of capitalism.

From the eighteenth century to the present day, industrialisation has given a powerful boost to growth; it has generated a remarkable increase in terms of both demography and consumption, and has recently reduced

© The Author(s) 2020

C. Perrotta, *Is Capitalism Still Progressive?*,
https://doi.org/10.1007/978-3-030-48169-8_7

poverty and famine. And yet industrialisation has also produced pollution of the environment, destruction of natural resources, the extinction of many living species, and global warming. With the welfare state the way seemed open for a decisive step forward to post-industrial production, which would have reduced these negative consequences of development to a minimum (see Sect. 5.1). This is not the way things went; indeed, the Western economic crisis is threatening to destroy the social cohesion of the democracies.

However, these same processes can, with the right approach, set development moving again. But it must be a new kind of development (see Chap. 8), making the logic of profit compatible with the common good,[1] and generating—alongside profit—other lines of development, based on human capital, greater social justice and remediation of the environment.

7.1 The Destruction of the Environment

7.1.1 *Industrialization, Demographic Growth and Increased Consumption*

Capitalistic accumulation has never been respectful of the environment. Until the last century, indiscriminate exploitation of the environment had been justified with the anthropocentric view of the universe characteristic of humanism, taking the environment to be in the service of humanity and its progress (see Sect. 1.2.2). Natural resources seemed to be unlimited. Air and water were the classical examples of vital assets with no economic value, being available in unlimited quantities. There was no awareness of pollution or harm to the environment.

Widescale destruction of the environment began with industrial production, which is the greatest upshot of capitalism but also reveals its "contradictory" nature. In its struggle for survival, humankind has been all too successful in destroying resources that support life. Between 1970 and 2014 consumption of land and forests destroyed 60% of the vertebrate species. Human activity is jeopardising the biodiversity that lies at the basis of human life on the earth.[2]

Poverty and famine have plagued humanity from its very beginnings. Today the partial victory over famine, which began in north-western

[1] For a similar approach, see Lippit (2005, chs. 7 and 8).
[2] WWF (2019: 6–7).

Europe, has led to a powerful demographic surge. According to the demographers, in 10,000 BC the entire human race numbered 4 million; in the year 1 A.D., 190 million, but in 1800 close to a billion. By 1960 the figure had climbed to 3 billion, and today stands at 7.7 billion.[3] This acceleration of growth is unsustainable, even though Africa, Australia and America are still decidedly underpopulated. Africa went through a long demographic crisis due to the slave trade, massacres committed by the colonialists and prolonged backwardness. Today, however, it is showing the highest growth rate in the world. North America and Australia still have insufficient immigration.

Nevertheless, the rate of population increase is slowing down thanks to the demographic transition (see below). The growth rate peaked in the 1963 (+ 2.2%), since then it has halved. By the end of the century the population will stand at around 11 billion, which should be the maximum arrived at even in the future. By then, the European population will have dropped by 100 million, while Latin America will have grown by only around 40 million, but Africa will have soared from the present 1.3 billion to 4.3 billion. Asia, on the other hand, should show little change, China losing nearly half a billion and India showing more limited growth, from the present 1.3 billion to 1.5 billion.[4]

In the early years of the twentieth century began—due to the rich and middle classes—what is known as the demographic transition: the families that had achieved a certain well-being, and with it an adequate culture, tended to defend the status they had arrived at by having fewer children and taking more care of them. Today the demographic transition has extended to China and India, but has yet to touch on Africa and Southeast Asia.

Demographic increase also depends on life expectancy, which increased very considerably in the twentieth century. Infant mortality rates plunged, as did the mortality rates of women giving birth and those due to infectious diseases and poor hygiene (see Sect. 1.3). In the backward countries this improvement came about far more quickly than it had in the West as a result not of economic development but rather of healthcare brought in from beyond their borders.

[3] OWD-World Population Growth.
[4] OWD-World Population Growth.

Malthusian apprehensions about population increase were rekindled at the end of the nineteenth century, with Wicksell,[5] and again in the mid-twentieth century. In 1948 the American author William Vogt published *Road to Survival*, which inspired the book by Paul R. Ehrlich, *The Population Bomb*, which came out in 1968. Eventually came *The limits to Growth* (1972), published by the Club di Roma—founded by Aurelio Peccei—written by a team of American scholars. The approach adopted in all these studies is tellingly summed up in "Project on the Predicament of Mankind", again due to the Club di Roma:

> The intent of the project is to examine the complex of problems troubling men of all nations: poverty in the midst of plenty; degradation of the environment; loss of faith in institutions; uncontrolled urban spread; insecurity of employment; alienation of youth; rejection of traditional values; and inflation and other monetary and economic disruptions.[6]

The passage quoted above could be repeated today word for word. A holistic vision is presented, in which all the factors interrelate and interact. Although these studies caused a stir at some levels, they had no appreciable influence on governments or enterprises. Resources are still being squandered. Technological progress lowered the cost of production, and this led to the culture of throwaway products.

7.1.2 Air, Water and Ground Pollution

With the use of wood and coal for fuel the air was already being polluted, but things got far worse with the first industrial cities—in Great Britain. Industrial power came from coal, emitting sulphur dioxide, nitric oxide, fine particulate matter (often formed by the combination of these two gases) and various other harmful gases.

So far pollution has gone ahead with scant monitoring and very few limitations. Only the last few decades have seen the obligation introduced to apply filters to chimneys and control toxic refuse disposal, but often control is too lax in the West, and practically non-existent elsewhere. In China and India both traditional domestic and industrial pollution are extremely widespread, and the annual mortality rate for ozone and

[5] Wicksell (1901: 214).

[6] Club of Rome (1972, Foreword: 10).

particulate matter emission exceeds a million in each of these countries.[7] The megalopolises with the worst pollution are in the poor countries (Delhi). An emblematic case is the disaster of Bhopal, in India in 1984, when a gas leak from the Union Carbide plant killed about 15,000 people and injured another half million (compensation for the casualties was paltry, remediation non-existent).

Today there are still many cases of deaths and children born with deformities in rich countries with limited public control, like the USA and Italy, due to asbestos dust, pollution from iron and steel works, oil refining, chemical and plastic production, and so on. Liquid refuse is often poured illegally into watercourses or lakes, poisoning the surrounding environment. Solid refuse is often illegally buried or burned. These activities have led to the burgeoning of eco-mafias. In the backward and emerging countries where democracy is wanting the situation is even worse, given the total lack of control. Very often noxious waste is—legally or illegally—sent to the poor countries, with devastating consequences.

As from the second half of the nineteenth century, the world of industry saw the addition of industrial agriculture, based on chemical products, the long-term effects of which have proved disastrous: the land becomes sterile, the groundwater, rivers and lakes are polluted. The use of chemical fertilisers (nitrogen compounds, phosphates, potassium) saw rapid advance throughout the twentieth century. By 1999 it had reached nearly 500 kg per hectare (kg/ha) in Holland, and 300 in the United Kingdom. Since then it has begun to be more limited, but remains very high at over 200 kg/ha in most of the developed countries. And there is no such limitation in China and India, both exceeding 500 kg/ha in 2015. In Ireland the figure stood at 561 kg/ha, in Egypt 645, in Colombia 670, while Singapore actually exceeded 33,000 kg/ha. In 1961 the use of fertilisers in the world came to 33.5 million tonnes, but by 2014 it had risen to 208 million. Africa produces and consumes only 3% of these products, but it's hard to say whether this is a case for rejoicing.[8]

Glyphosate-based herbicides cause serious harm to animal organisms and human consumers, too, and in particular to the nervous system of children.[9] The use of pesticides in agriculture is now on a vast scale; they are used to protect crops from harmful animal or vegetal agents, but they

[7] OWD—Air pollution.
[8] World Bank and FAO data (see OWD—Food—Fertilizers and Pesticides).
[9] European Parliament—The Green-EFA-PAN (2017: 10–11).

poison the soil, the groundwater and the people who eat the vegetables sprayed with them. From 1990 to 2016 world consumption rose from 1.5 kg/ha to 2.57. Japan and Colombia consume over 14, Holland 14, and China 11.[10]

A fundamental factor for pollution lies in large-scale stock farming for the production of meat. This sector sees great concentration on the worldwide scale, reducing production to a few oligopolies. The animals suffer atrociously from the impossibility of moving around, the unnatural feeding times and the medicines (antibiotics, additives and hormones, besides the insecticides) which poison the consumer, too. The waste matter they produce is extremely toxic and pollutes the soil and groundwater.[11]

The destruction of our basic resources (air, water, earth) does not stop here. There is also the uncontrolled manipulation of food and drink. On top of all this comes destruction of the fauna in the environment, often due to premodern culture that is taking on disastrous aspects in the capitalistic market (extermination of asses, tigers and rhinoceroses for alleged therapeutic or aphrodisiac qualities,[12] of elephants for ivory,[13] and whales for hunting).

7.1.3 Plastic

With demographic increase and greater well-being the consumption of natural materials has grown enormously. With plastic, therefore, there is considerable saving in the use of materials like wood, rubber, glass and ceramic, while at the same time it enables the production of light, complex objects once unimaginable. However, the uncontrolled production and dispersion of it in the environment is causing untold damage.

Synthetic resins, called plastic, were invented for the precise purpose of being more longer-lasting than many other natural materials. But in the last few decades we have learnt that plastic takes hundreds of years to decay, while production of it is growing exponentially. Recycling plastic is technically difficult (and governments are not helping research in this

[10] FAOSTAT, online, "Pesticides".

[11] See Liberti (2016: 40, passim).

[12] From 100,000 at the beginning of the twentieth century the tiger population has now (2010) dropped to 3500 (corriere.it, 25/6/2010). The surviving rhinoceroses number 20,000 (*Guardian News* 2019 online).

[13] The number of elephants in the wild has fallen from 4 million in the twentieth century to 415,000. In the 1980s 100,000 a year were being killed (WWF 2019, online).

direction), exceeding 50% only in northern Europe. The rest is dispersed in the environment. It breaks down into micro-plastics (pieces smaller than 5 mm) which are ingested by marine wildlife, mistaking them for food, by many birds and, finally, by humans through the animals. In 2018 micro-plastics were found in 114 marine species.

Even if it is not dispersed in the environment, plastic causes pollution because it releases gases harmful for living organisms, occurring for example in packing material, certain automobile and computer components, cosmetics, perfumes and medical instruments. These materials damage hormonal balance and the endocrine system. Over the long term amphibians, molluscs and insects show damage to the reproductive apparatus and other alterations. The production of plastic had risen from about 1.5 million tonnes in 1950 to 400 million tonnes by 2015, and seems likely to have doubled by 2025. Today something between 5 and 14 million tonnes end up in the oceans. In the 1960s some scientists noticed the formation of islands of plastic in the oceans. In 2014 it was estimated that over 5000 billion plastic particles amounting to a total weight of 250,000 tonnes were floating on the surface of the oceans. They cluster in five subtropical gyres—two in the North and South Pacific, two in the North and South Atlantic, and one in the Indian Ocean.[14]

The developed countries are unable to dispose of a large proportion of plastic they produce. Until 2017 they exported it, mainly to China, but China is no longer accepting it. So the developed countries are paying to export plastic refuse to other countries (the USA exports 16.5% of the total, Japan 15.3%). The poor countries that accept it almost always burn it, releasing poisonous gases.[15]

7.2 Global Warming

7.2.1 *The Effects of Global Warming*

Another consequence of industrialisation is global warming. The use of energy obtained from fossil fuel (coal, oil and various gases) produces enormous quantities of carbon dioxide (CO2) and other gases, causing the greenhouse effect: the production of these gases has reached such a rate that the waters of the oceans, the atmosphere and the surface of the

[14] See Moore (2019).

[15] Alessandro Sala, in *Corriere della Sera*, 23 April 2019.

earth are falling behind in absorbing and recycling them. The unabsorbed gases occupy part of the atmosphere, forming a shield that prevents the surface of the earth from dispersing the excess heat of the sun, as in a greenhouse. So the environment continues warming up.

Besides, fossil fuels, cattle and pig farms, and even rice fields, produce methane, contributing to the increase in greenhouse gases. The major greenhouse gases are (in brackets see the respective percentages of emissions in 2015): carbon dioxide, CO2 (81.2), methane (10.6), nitrous oxide (5.5) and hydrofluorocarbons (2.5). There are also chlorofluorocarbons, produced artificially, which in the past caused the hole in the ozone layer letting in dangerous ultraviolet rays from the sun.

Before industrialisation, the carbon particles in the atmosphere came to far less than 300 ppm (parts per million), but now they exceed 400. Anti-greenhouse effect policies have brought down the rate of increase of ppm, but the absolute increase remains.[16] According to the IPCC (Intergovernmental Panel on Climate Change), 25% of greenhouse gas comes from the combustion of coal, oil and natural gases used to produce heat and electric energy; 24% comes from agriculture, stock farming and deforestation; 21% from industry, 14% from transport and 10% from residential or commercial use.

Calculating emissions on the basis of electricity production, the sector accounting for most (over 30%) comprises dwellings and businesses, with their heating, air-conditioning and consumption of electricity for various purposes. Then comes transport, with 29% of emissions, cars and motorcycles accounting for 59% of them. Stock farming produces 14% of the greenhouse gases—mainly methane—65% of which are due to cattle (the breeding farms for meat emit twice as much as the dairy farms), 9% to pigs and 8% to chickens. As for the countries, China comes first for emissions (28% of the total), followed by the USA (15%) and the EU (9%). For per capita production, the main oil producing countries of the Middle East top the list.[17]

Another source of pollution lies in rainforest fires and deforestation in general. Rainforests conserve carbon dioxide in the solid state in the soil and plants; they also contain a very high level of biodiversity. Their destruction releases CO2 and lowers the level of biodiversity, destroying many animal and plant species. The fires in Amazonia and Congo, like the felling

[16] Morgan and Fullbrook (2019: 2).
[17] *Il Post* 14/9/2019, online.

of trees in Borneo, and so on serve to take over land, collecting the timber or growing crops but, above all (in 80% of the cases) to create pastureland, given the growing demand for meat. It is the multinationals, above all, that are guiding the destruction of the rainforests, almost always with help from the states.[18] In Brazilian Amazonia, 2019 (up to September) saw 73,000 fires serving the purpose of deforestation (85% more than the year before). Many burnt areas were territory of the indigenous population. Despite the genocides, there are still hundreds of thousands of natives in Amazonia, divided into 400 tribes, each with its cultural heritage, now risking disappearance.[19] In Congo, China has taken over from Europe in the systematic destruction of the rainforest to obtain timber.[20]

Global warming of just one degree is having disastrous effects. In the first place, it is melting the glaciers and icecaps. Melting glaciers mean a reduction in the water feeding the rivers, and thus a reduction in evaporation and increasing desertification. The melting of the polar icecaps is raising the level of the oceans, which have already submerged various islands in the Pacific and are threatening coastal towns. With global warming the permafrost of the coldest areas of the earth is melting, with consequent release of great quantities of CO2, which had been captured by the frozen ground.

As a result of air and water warming, the temperate zones are being invaded by tropical insects, fish and molluscs. This is disturbing the biological cycles of plants and crops; it is fading the coral, and causing an alternation of drought and increasingly violent hurricanes, even in the temperate zones. This alternation is impoverishing agriculture and leading to famine, desertification and flooding. To limit warming to 1.5° the CO2 emissions of 2010 need to have been reduced by 45% by 2030.[21]

As in the case of pollution, also for global warming the poorest areas of the planet are paying the highest price. The 50% poorer population of the world contributes only 10% to the total lifestyle consumption emissions, but suffer more than the others for the consequences. The contribution of the richest 10%, on the other hand, amounts to 49% (and they have ways and means to protect themselves from the resulting harm).[22] Climate

[18] For the Congo, see *Nigrizia*, 29/6/2018.

[19] *Quartz* (USA online newspaper) 22/8/2019.

[20] See Marta Gatti, "Legno africano per il 'made in China'", *Nigrizia* 5/10/2018.

[21] IPCC Report, Press Release, 8 Oct. 2018, online.

[22] *Real-World Economics Review Blog*, August 5, 2019, Oxfam 2015 data.

change puts the progress made by the poorer countries over the last 50 years at risk of being reversed, reducing 120 million people to poverty by 2030.[23]

7.2.2 Denialism

Scientists have been calling for a halt to global warming with increasing urgency. In 1992 an appeal was signed by 1700 scientists while a further appeal was signed by over 15,000 experts from 184 countries in 2017.[24] Periodically meetings are being held at the worldwide level to reduce CO2 emissions, beginning with the Rio de Janeiro meeting in 1992. Some of these conferences have arrived at agreements among countries (besides the Rio meeting, Kyoto 2005 and Paris 2018 were particularly successful in this respect). On the basis of the agreements reached, policies have been launched to curb emissions, but with limited effects. For decades the worst polluters—the USA and China—have turned their backs on the agreements. The USA recognised them with Obama, but pulled out once again with Trump. China finally fell in and sought to expand the sources of clean energy (wind, solar, etc.), but then, realising how costly it was to invest in clean energy, fell back to setting up scores of new coal-based power stations.

So far policy at the worldwide level has failed to halt the greenhouse effect. The world consumption of clean energy has become significant only in this century: nearly 1000 TWh with wind energy (one terawatt hour = a billion kWh), 333 with solar energy and over 1800 with other sources of renewable energy. However, in 2016 coal consumption reached 43,000 TWh, and oil consumption 53,000.[25] As for the EU, in 1990–2017 emissions of sulphur dioxide were reduced by 90%, of particulate matter by 50%, and of greenhouse gas by 22%. Nevertheless, in 2017 EU consumption of coal still stood at around 7.2 tonnes per capita.[26]

Fighting global warming is a slow and difficult business due to the many interests of producers and consumers. In the 1960s intensive propaganda denying global warming was unleashed in the USA. Scientists in the pay of oil tycoons lent their support to the denialist arguments, which

[23] Beuret (2019).

[24] For the 2017 appeal, see *Sbilanciamoci*, 27/XI/2017, online.

[25] OWD, Energy—Energy production.

[26] Eurostat, Environment—Air pollution.

found ample exposure in the media. These activities are still obstructing policies against global warming.[27] Syll (2019) accuses the IPCC of advising governments on the basis of the Nordhaus models. Such models, he holds, use a "spurious method" to argue that we should not be too worried about global warming if it doesn't come to more than 3.5° above preindustrial levels. Even worse is the position taken by the American Environmental Protection Agency in May 2018, with the declaration that burning forests is to be considered "carbon neutral" since an equal number of trees can be replanted. This official position will weaken the obstacles to deforestation.[28]

The big multinationals have now realised that it is in their own interest to accept the principle of public interest ensuring guarantees both for the environment and for future profits. Indeed, they are now going into the production and use of green energy, but at the same time they are continuing with the use of hydrocarbons. This compromise is good for profits but, slowing down change, it risks leading us to disaster.

7.3 Emigration and the Crisis of Social Cohesion

For about 20 years the flow of migration to the rich countries has been swelling exponentially. It has been estimated that the number of emigrants from the poor to the developed countries did not exceed 35 million between 1950 and 1989.[29] Between 2000 and 2019, however, the presence of migrants in the world increased from 2.8% of the population to 3.5%, coming close to 272 million. Of these, over 83 million were in Asia, and nearly as many in Europe, over 70 million in the Americas, and 26.5 million in Africa. Of the emigrants present in Europe, 50 million are in the Mediterranean area and the North West. And 50.7 million of the migrants in the Americas are in the USA. After the USA, the countries with the highest intake of migrants are Germany and Saudi Arabia, with 13 million each, followed by Russia (11.6 million) and the United Kingdom (9.6 million).[30] Emigration for environmental reasons is also

[27] See e.g. Stiglitz (2019).

[28] See GDAE (Global Development and Environment Institute), Tufts University (USA), May 2018.

[29] Bairoch (1997, ch. 32: 1342).

[30] IOM (International Organization on Migrations), online.

increasing, with people fleeing from areas ruined by climate change and desertification.

As we know, the flow of migrants is not proportional to the level of poverty of the country of origin. In fact, there must be a minimum of development for emigration to begin. Today emigration towards the rich countries is due not only to economic but also to cultural motives. The Western life model (which includes rights, guarantees, meritocratic practices and opportunities to study) is now sought after in the poor countries, too, thanks in part to digital information. Those who have any chance seek escape from poverty, but also from the violence and insecurity, or indeed oppression, of certain regimes.

Another powerful motive for emigration derives from the demographic gap. In Europe and Japan the birth rate is too low, the population is progressively ageing and there are no longer enough young people to keep the elderly with their work. Thus a strong force of attraction for emigrants lies in the demand for labour shown by the developed economies. On the other hand, there is a demographic explosion in Africa (but also in the Middle East, Afghanistan and Pakistan) with growth rates of between 2% and 3%. 23 African countries have a per capita annual income of less than a thousand dollars, while in Nigeria and Senegal—which both show high rates of emigration towards Europe—per capita income stands respectively at around \$2000 and \$1400.[31]

Demographic growth in Africa is unsustainable for both the economy and the environment, while also holding back development. However, if the present trend continues demographic transition should begin to set in around 2050. The Africans arriving in Europe account for only 12% of Africa's emigrants, while 82% (nearly 20 million) are accounted for by emigration within the continent (2017).[32] Often internal migrations are forced, and dominated by traffickers in human beings.

In the West there is a shortage of low-skilled workers in the sector of services and material labour. Here the demand for labour on the part of both enterprises and consumers of personal services (caregivers, housemaids, security and cleaning staff, etc.) remains unsatisfied. Western young people do not cover these areas because, given their qualifications after years of study and their living standards, they would not receive an adequate salary. Even if they do accept such jobs, they fail to achieve

[31] WorldData.info—Income, online.

[32] Antonella Sinopoli, "Flusso inarrestabile", *Nigrizia* 14 September 2018.

economic independence. Thus a segmented labour market has formed in the developed countries, with two sectors virtually cut off from one another (v. VI.1). This is why the EU somewhat reductively states that "In destination countries, international migration may be used as a tool to solve specific labour market shortages."[33]

The double labour market exists in the West because—after 40 years—we have yet to complete transition to the post-industrial economy, which calls for a great increase in immaterial production both in the form of growth of human capital (research, training, specialisation, culture, organisation, projects, and so forth) and in the form of new artisanal or executive labour, able to use the new materials and technologies. Both these fields of labour show difficulty in expanding in the West. So it is that about half the Western young people with qualifications, as well as the immigrants, are driven to jobs with low productivity and poor pay. And the vast majority of the enterprises themselves are still unprepared for the post-industrial economy: instead of creating new types of jobs, they prefer to exploit the widespread unemployment to force people into unskilled, low-paid jobs. Hence the huge proliferation of insecure jobs, often performed at relentless rates (some obvious examples are home delivery in the cities, piece-rate work in rural areas). Failure to move on to a more advanced economy is harming everyone, whether or not they have studied, whether Westerners or immigrants.

The longer the immobilism of the western economy lasts, the more perverse effects it has on social cohesion. And yet the immobilism is caused by defence of the privileges generated by the crisis. It is not only the billionaires, multinationals and entrepreneurs exploiting insecure labour that have accumulated privileges, but also the middle class that evades taxes or at any rate has achieved a degree of well-being it is afraid of losing (see Sect. 6.2.2). All these classes, which in some cases make up a good half of society, see migrants as a destabilising factor that threatens their security, and consequently point them out as the cause of crisis and the shortage of jobs.

On the other side we have the unprotected—poor or at risk of unemployment, young people with meagre incomes, or artisans, shopkeepers and small entrepreneurs facing an uncertain future. These unprotected classes are all too easily taken in by the demagogy of the protected classes: they seek refuge in visions of security and strong identity, pursuing the

[33] Eurostat, Migration and Migrant Population Statistics, March 2019, online.

fetish of distinction by religion, "race" and nation, and hating the élites, science, intermediary entities and competencies. Funke et al. (2016) hold that from 1870 on, every crisis resulting from financial speculation has been followed by a sharp swerve of the electorate towards the far right, which attributes the crisis to minorities or foreigners.

In the years of the welfare state it was generally believed that the conquests achieved by capitalism in terms of civilisation would never be lost. Today we are not so sure. The fabric holding Western society together is fraying, thereby threatening its values and setting many citizens adrift from the principles of solidarity and civic education. The resulting situation is much like what the sociologist Banfield (1958) called "amoral familism", that is the tendency to view the world as hostile and limit moral values to the protection of self and family. Significantly, however, what Banfield was analysing was an extremely poor, premodern society in the South of Italy, which suggests that we are sliding far back in our attitudes.

The situation is even worse outside North-Western Europe. In almost all the countries of Asia and Eastern Europe the room to exercise civil and human rights is increasingly cramped, while those who defend them face persecution. But it is yet worse in Latin America, Africa and the Middle East, where persecution aiming at these rights often takes violent forms, and those who assert them risk falling victim to criminal activity. All too often this is also the case with religious, political and sexual minorities. In the Middle East, India and Africa women's rights are repressed, often with violence.[34]

Ultimately, the economic and social crisis of the West is transforming the inflow of migrants from a factor of great value for development into a culturally explosive factor that is depleting the scope for democracy.

References

Amnesty International (2018) *Report 2017/18*, online.

Bairoch, Paul (1997) *Storia economica e sociale del mondo*, trans. of *Victoires et déboires. Histoire économique et sociale du monde du XVIe siècle à nos jours*, Torino: Einaudi, 1999.

Banfield, Edward C. (1958) *Basi morali di una società arretrata*, trans. from English, Bologna: il Mulino, 2006.

Beuret, Nicholas (2019) "Emissions Inequality ...", *Social Europe*, April 10.

[34] *Amnesty International* (2018: 418–463).

Club of Rome. (1972) *The Limits to Growth*, New York: Universe Books, by Meadows, Donella et al.

European Parliament—The Green-EFA-PAN. (2017) Alternatives to Herbicide Use in Weed Management. The Case of Glyphosate, online.

Funke, Manuel, M. Schularick, C. Trebesch (2016) "Going to Extremes: Politics After Financial Crises, 1870–2014", *European Economic Review*, Sept. 2016: 227–260.

Liberti, Stefano (2016) *I signori del cibo*, Roma: Minimum Fax.

Lippit, Victor (2005) *Capitalism*, London and New York: Routledge.

Moore, Charles (2019) "Plastic pollution", *Encyclopaedia Britannica*, online.

Morgan, Jamie and Fullbrook, Edward (2019) "Introduction: Economics and Civilization in Ecological Crisis", *Real-World Economics Review*, 87: 2–8.

OWD (Our World in Data), ed. Max Roser, online: https://ourworldindata.org/

Stiglitz, Joseph (2019) "Corporate Greed Is Accelerating Climate Change …", *CNN Business*, April 21.

Syll, Lars (2019) "Nordhaus Dangerous Gamble for Humanity's Future", *Real-World Economics Review Blog*, Sept. 21.

Wicksell, Knut (1901) *Lectures on Political Economy*, trans. from Swedish, vol. 1, Fairfield: Kelley, 1977; online Von Mises inst.

WWF (World Wildlife Fund) (2019) *Living Planet Report 2018*, online.

CHAPTER 8

Labour-Based Development

Abstract The data attest to remarkable social improvement in the world, but the gaps between the rich countries and the others are still huge, and conditions are worsening for the poorer countries. Today three models of capitalism prevail. The European model upholds human rights, but it remains based on neo-colonialism. The Chinese model promotes development in the ex-colonies, but continues to plunder their resources, and above all it is no friend of democracy—its paternalism seems incompatible with the culture of the middle class. The populist antidemocratic model, on the other hand, is a product of neoliberalism. It is up to the Europeans, now, to protect labour and employment, embark on large-scale investment to restore the environment and help the poor and emerging countries on the way to development.

Keywords World growth • Capitalist models • China • Labour • Green New Deal

8.1 World Growth and Its Limits

8.1.1 The Present Trends

Since 1990 the world has seen some significant improvements. 2.6 billion people have gained access to drinking water. Annual infant mortality (under the age of 5) has halved, from 12.7 to 6.3 million. Primary school

© The Author(s) 2020

C. Perrotta, *Is Capitalism Still Progressive?*,
https://doi.org/10.1007/978-3-030-48169-8_8

admission, including girls, has become almost universal. Extreme poverty—less than 2 dollars per capita a day—has diminished by 1% a year (although as from 2013 the rate of reduction has fallen by 40%).[1] From 1960 to 2015 the level of world literacy rose from 42% to 86%, although in many countries (Somalia, Zaire, Nigeria, Mali, Afghanistan, etc.) the schools have often come under attack, the students killed. The wide generation gap shows how much progress has been made: in Algeria, 16% of the over 65-year-olds are literate, but 92% of the young people between the ages of 15 and 24. In Saudi Arabia the percentages are, respectively, 26% and 90%; in Iran, 22% and 99%.[2]

World life expectancy—no more than 32 years in 1800—had reached 48 years by 1950, and 70 years by 2012, while in the developed countries it now stands at 81–83 years.[3] In Africa, however, it still comes short of 63 years.[4] Child labour has seen a steady decrease as from the mid-twentieth century. In 2012, 17% of children in the world were working, but just 2–3% in the more advanced countries. Women have been taking a larger share of the labour market almost everywhere, thereby enjoying increasing autonomy. Since 1980 the consumption of fresh water has remained unchanged for the OECD countries, but it has increased by over 50% in the rest of the world.[5]

And yet the distances between the developed countries and the others remain enormous. The per capita GDP of the rich countries has shown steady growth since 1980; in 2016 it came between $40,000 and $50,000 (while in Africa it was less than $5000, and in other areas between $10,000 and $20,000).[6] After the crisis of 2008, the rich countries bounced back to the previous GDP levels, but the other countries have yet to do so (including China, but with the exception of India). Per capita GDP is falling in Latin America and Africa.[7] In 2018 the total wealth had grown from the previous year in China (4.6%), Africa (4.4%) and India (2.6%), but the developed countries saw a greater increase: 6.5% in North America,

[1] Oxfam (2019: 10–27).
[2] UNESCO and OECD data (see OWD, Education—Literacy).
[3] OWD, Population—Life expectancy, 2019.
[4] Eurostat, Population & Health, 2019.
[5] OWD—Child labor, —Female Labor Supply, —Water Use and Stress, 2019.
[6] OWD—Economic Growth.
[7] FAO (2019, fig. 22) and World Bank Development Indicators, online.

and 5% in Europe, but in Latin America it decreased by 4.9% (the only negative figure).[8]

Poverty continues to afflict the most backward areas. World malnutrition had fallen from the 15% of the population in 2000 to 10.6% by 2015, but it is now increasing again. It is still suffered by 21.3% of the population of sub-Saharan Africa and 15.6% of the population of southern Asia, and it is on the rise in the poorest countries, above all in Africa.[9] As for malnourished children, in China the percentage decreased sharply between 1992 and 2015 (from 30% to 8%) and in India (from 70% to 38.4%), but in Africa the percentage now exceeds 40%.[10]

In 2015 the mortality rate of women due to childbirth in the countries of Europe ranged between 3 and 9 per 100,000 children born (14 in the USA). In the developing countries, however, it is still very high: 174 in India, 206 in Bolivia, 693 in Zaire. Finally, Africa and southern Asia are still plagued by malaria and tetanus (see Sect. 1.3). In South Africa 18% of the population between the ages of 15 and 49 have succumbed to HIV.[11] To be added to this grim list is the scourge of Ebola, for which the American Food and Drug Administration has, however, just approved a vaccine.[12]

There are still some significant data to consider. In sub-Saharan Africa 32% of the population as yet have no access to drinking water, and 65% have no access to electricity.[13] In 2015, the annual per capita consumption of energy came to 44,400 TWh in Germany, but in China it came to 26,000, and in India 7400.[14] Finally, Piketty estimates that in Africa 40–50% of manufacturing is in foreign hands.[15]

8.1.2 The Factors for Growth

The first factor for growth of the ex-colonies lies in Chinese foreign investments. China is helping various countries in Africa, Latin America and

[8] Credit Suisse (2019) "The world generated $ 14 trillion in wealth last year", 5 charts, online, chart 1.

[9] FAO and OWD—Food-Hunger, 2019.

[10] FAO (2019).

[11] OWD, Health—Maternal mortality and Health—HIV.

[12] See *Quartz*, Dec. 20, 2019.

[13] Oxfam (2019: 19).

[14] OWD, Energy—Energy production. TWh: terawatt hours.

[15] Piketty (2014: 68–69).

Southeast Asia to make large-scale investments, with long-period facilitated loans. It is also making direct investments to exploit the natural resources of these areas.[16] In fact, Chinese development is crying out for raw materials: coal, oil, timber, minerals, land, water, food, etc.[17] For Asia and Europe, Chinese policy has found a global container in the great project of the new Silk Road ("One belt one road" or "Belt and Road Initiative").

Another major factor for growth lies in the rapid development of the digital economy launched by the USA, which sees the collaboration of the developed countries plus China and India. The digital technologies represent a driving force for the present production of wealth and are transforming labour and the economy in all the countries (see below, section 3).

The third factor for growth lies in the transfer of resources—largely from the West—on a vast scale to the poor countries carried out by UNO, tens of thousands of NGOs (funded by private parties), private foundations and various other bodies involved in activities of solidarity. Beginning with *Millennium Goals*, UNO has been exerting moral suasion on the rich countries and implementing—in some cases directly through its agencies—ambitious policies to provide assistance and fight epidemics, famine and illiteracy.[18] In addition, there are also the traditional good works of Christian churches and Islamic associations promoting health and education together with various other micro-projects. Finally, many universities in the rich countries are training young people from poor countries so that they can return to their places of origin and get them moving in the direction of development. The importance of the third factor should not be underrated. These resources are being used for the development of poor countries in a vast range of fields, from village micro-projects (e.g. for water) to education, peacekeeping, creation of administrative structures, and so on.

For years this aid has been coming in for criticism as a source of corruption.[19] It is in fact fair criticism when the aid is deceptive, provided to gain political control over a country or to open the way for the multinationals. This alleged aid corrupts the élites of the various countries because

[16] For data on Chinese foreign investments, see the Boston University *Global Development Policy Center* Newsletter.

[17] See Moyo (2012).

[18] See Vaggi (2018, ch. 2).

[19] See e.g. Moyo (2009). Deaton (2013, ch. 7).

it exposes them to uncontrolled exploitation of their natural resources. However, neo-colonial policies of the kind have nothing to do with the aid we have been considering. One example among many of necessary help is when it serves to slow down demographic growth in Africa, which threatens to nip development in the bud. If action isn't taken, by 2050 nearly 90% of the population south of the Sahara will be in conditions of poverty. Various campaigns have been launched by NGOs and foundations to inform young women about birth control.[20]

Despite these considerable factors for growth, there is no generalised development on the worldwide scale. On the whole, the growth processes have produced such extreme inequalities that most of the wealth is being channelled towards parasitic rents (through speculation or hoarding).

8.2 Three Models of Capitalism

The world economy now largely rests on three different models of capitalism, which are competing for hegemony.

8.2.1 The European Model

The first is the European Union model which—at least in its proclamations—promotes enlightened ideals: equality before the law, rights of ownership and entrepreneurship, freedom of conscience and speech and, in short, democracy. Countless times these ideals have been betrayed by the Europeans themselves, but at least they have been reasserted and today are, to some extent, guiding EU policies, weak as they may be. Enlightened social thinking is based on the assumption that economic well-being, freedom and true civilisation can only grow together, not apart.

In the course of history European capitalism has created a solid basis of material well-being, which—despite a long series of errors and horrors—has helped bring out the best of certain aspects of human nature: the aspiration for individual freedom, for enrichment or success, as well as the need to have one's merits recognised. European capitalism has regulated and set the limits to these tendencies through the impersonal mechanism of competition and with the legal system of guarantees and division of powers. Finally, thanks to well-being individuals, groups and institutions

[20] Anna Loschiavo, "Corsa ad ostacoli", *Nigrizia Notizie*, 24 September 2018.

have been able to engage in an impressively large number of projects to promote solidarity.

The enlightened approach that associated material well-being with freedom and civil progress re-emerged during the boom of the welfare state. It was in this setting that the generation of baby-boomers appeared on the scene. But eventually the setting started to crumble. All three processes of growth (economic, civil and democratic) are now coming up against increasing difficulties. Europe is contradicting its own ideals, pursuing policies of neo-colonial exploitation, closing its doors on migrants fleeing from inhuman situations and showing scant zeal in defending the environment.

Nevertheless, the EU is the only great power defending democracy, repudiating war and aggression, and seeking—albeit somewhat intermittently—to set limits to the excessive power of the big corporations. This makes it all the more attractive to populations in conditions of poverty and oppression. Only the European model is able to achieve a new form of economic and human development in freedom. To do so, however, Europe must get its economy moving and relaunch development on the basis of employment and human capital.

Europe has to get its welfare state back in place,[21] and promote a number of major projects including unification of fiscal policies and restoration of progressive taxation.[22] To boost productivity it needs to raise wages[23] (now lower than they were before the 2008 crisis).[24] It needs to fight tax evasion and avoidance, address immigration by finding jobs for the newcomers, narrow the European generation gap and cope with the crisis of social security contributions; it must programme conversion of manufacture production, promote growth of the digital economy, fight global warming by turning to new energy sources, and restore the environment.

8.2.2 Chinese Capitalism

The second model is to be found in China, which sees democracy as a western product alien to its history. The Chinese state has always dominated society with a paternalistic approach, granting scant freedom (see

[21] See e.g. Vanhercke et al. (2018).

[22] Piketty and Vauchez (2018).

[23] See *Benchmarking Working Europe* 2019, chs. 2 and 3.

[24] Coulter (2019).

Sect. 1.1.3).[25] Despite its self-proclaimed communism, over the last 40 years China has made room for the capitalistic market and self-interest, creating a complex economic and financial structure. Nevertheless, the political élite has retained authoritarian control over society. Chinese capitalism is proving decidedly successful, thanks in part to certain undesirable factors. Wages are low, the currency is undervalued with respect to the west, the state exerts strict control, violations of the rules and honest principles of the market are frequent, and the environment is being ruined with practically no control.[26]

As we have seen (see Sect. 8.1.2), to its considerable credit China has promoted development for the backward countries, although they pay for this aid by giving over their natural resources in return and standing by as their environment is ravaged.[27] Madagascar is a case in point, albeit an extreme one. This country, where 90% of the population is in absolute poverty (living on less than two dollars a day) is one of the few that are regressing. The Chinese are consuming their rainforest and fish resources, while illiteracy has increased from 30% to 50%.[28]

It is worth noting, too, that China is also a world leader in the most advanced technologies, has an excellent educational system and is generous in its contributions to research and the creation of great infrastructures; wages are rising, the middle classes growing. One may well wonder whether these middle classes will continue to accept a police state that controls even the smallest details of their private lives, punishes political criticism and freedom of opinion with extreme severity and persecutes the religious minorities. In Europe, freedom was a conquest of the middle classes, while universal suffrage and democracy came later thanks mainly to the lower classes. Is something of the sort likely to happen in China?

If not, how will China behave with its economic allies? Will it accept the fact that they are free and democratic, or will it subject them to authoritarian government? Is the "liberation of the Third World" going to become a new Orwellian nightmare, or, like Hong Kong today, will it become a thorn in the flesh of Chinese totalitarianism?

[25] See Castronovo (2011: 116–132).

[26] On the destruction of the environment, see R. Smith (2017).

[27] See for Africa Donou-Adonsou (2018) and for Latin America, Salazar-Xirinachs (2019, ch. 1).

[28] See Rachele Gonnelli in *Sbilanciamoci* 17 January 2019.

8.2.3 *From Neoliberalism to the New Populism*

The third model of capitalism is in fact a degeneration of the European model brought on by neoliberalism (which is democratic only in purely formal terms). Today, all too many governments pay homage to formal democracy but in practice fall back on antidemocratic systems and theorise the antiliberal state. Russia, Poland, Hungary, Turkey and Brazil and many other countries now have governments that are legitimised by elections but which, in practice, tend to gag free speech, controlling the press and the media, seeking to bring the judiciary under their sway, concentrating economic power to the advantage of their coteries, setting no limits to devastation of the environment or oppression of the workers and bringing illegal means to bear against the propaganda of the opposition and the action of the intermediate institutions.

These governments implicitly legitimise the many oppressive regimes there are in the world. The "non-liberal" model itself is defended by minority nationalist forces in a number of European and American democracies. It is the model that harks back to many aspects of history's populist or fascist governments, from the rule of Charles-Louis-Napoléon Bonaparte in France in the 1860s to the European and South American fascist regimes of the 1920s–1930s and on, up to Perón. In these regimes the leader addresses the people directly, calling for plebiscitary consensus; the movements rebel against the élites, whatever form they take. Such regimes appeal to the irrational, emotional instincts and eschew critical analysis.

Populism, too, like the Chinese model, is a far cry from the enlightened conception of development. If the European model were to give way, the Western world would fall under a mass of populist regimes and something very much like the Fascism of the 1920s and 1930s would triumph once again.

8.3 What Does the New Development Consist In?

8.3.1 *Neoliberal Myths and Employment Strategies*

To bring about a new phase of development a number of false myths must first be exposed—the myth that immobilism is preferable to change, the myth—converging with the former one—that society organised in corporations is a good solution, and, finally, the myth—previously considered at the historical level (II.2.d)—that growth can be achieved with the market alone, without the state.

As for the first myth, we need to abandon Vilfredo Pareto's false axiom that change is positive only if it means that "some are better off and no one else is worse off". In reality, any change will always go against some interests. To save the environment we need to reduce the use of coal and oil, which means reducing the profits of those who produce them and the advantages of those who use them. If public transport is made more efficient the earnings of private transport companies will be so much the less, and so forth. Everyone is aware of these obvious facts except the economists who believe in Pareto's axiom (i.e. the vast majority).

As for the second myth, social cohesion is not to be misinterpreted as the harmonious coexistence of groups with corporative interests. Corporative society shaped in the West during the long semi-stagnation following on from the crisis of the welfare state, and is still in place. One effect that stagnation regularly gives rise to is the crystallisation of groups whose interests set them against change; despite the rivalry between them, they are united in the defence of their privileges, whether legitimate or illicit.[29] This Holy Alliance consists of all sorts of groups: the classes enjoying the greatest wealth, the multinationals, manufacturers who produce pollution, tax evaders, the entrepreneurs-clients of the state, a good part of the public administration, the professional corporations and the classes benefiting from assistance. Corporative society is biased in favour of welfarism and rents, and averse to free competition and the criterion of merit.

The third myth has it that the fewer the rules are, the more the economy grows. In reality, the new line of development will emerge only with firm guidance by the institutions, working for the public interest. For example, left without control the technological revolution is creating widespread unemployment, the digital divide (the gap between those who can use the digital tools and those who can't), a new proletariat, marginalisation and social aggressiveness. Only the supranational organisations and the national states can turn this mechanism threatening disaster into a virtuous process.

The institutions have the means to assert the criterion of social wellbeing. To do so, however, they must stop being culturally subordinate to neoliberalism and must launch a vigorous public investment policy—stimulating private investment—for productive employment. Public policies

[29] See e.g. Moe (2007: 25).

must go in three directions: supporting labour and enhancing human capital, taking environmental remediation in hand, and sketching out a development plan for the poor countries.

The new development strategy will have to be global; it will have to reappraise all the sectors at all levels. It must disinter the target of the post-Keynesians in the 1950s–1960s, namely full employment. Work is a right, and it coincides with the right to a decent existence.[30] It is now all too evident that capitalistic accumulation can go no further as long as it excludes a good part of humanity from well-being. The new development strategy is bound to fail if contraposition persists between the advanced and developing countries, between secure old and insecure young generations.

8.3.2 Priority for Work

To reverse the neoliberal regression labour rights must be staunchly defended, punishing those who directly or indirectly make use of slave or semi-slave labour (whether multinationals or small farms), setting a minimum wage, ensuring equal pay between men and women, providing efficient public services, protecting the weaker categories of workers, putting a decided stop to work for school-aged young people and preventing school dropout. Collective bargaining should be made obligatory as it protects the weakest. Violation of labour rights harms not only the workers, but also the economy as a whole since it acts as a disincentive for competition based on increased productivity and thwarts the development of human capital.[31]

On the other hand, the public administration needs to show efficiency, promoting development rather than obstructing it. On the evidence of many studies, a polarisation is underway between highly specialised and elementary work, while the room for medium-skilled work is shrinking.[32] This state of affairs can be tackled only by speeding up transition to the post-industrial economy, in which increase in wealth is based on growth of human capital. The fundamental factors for human capital are increase in employment and in education and training. *Today the way to get*

[30] Pollin (2012). Komlos (2018).

[31] iASES (2019, ch. 2). In 2019 many of the articles in *Social Europe* stressed this need.

[32] See e.g. Madi (2017).

development moving again lies in replacing a good part of the traditional, relatively unproductive jobs with new, productive jobs.[33]

The post-industrial economy can free profit from the despotic role it took on with neoliberalism. We must shake off the obsession with growth at all costs. It is positive only when the investments enhance the conditions of society. The rise of capitalism rested on the capacity to reconcile private interests with the public interest (see Chap. 2). Today there is only one way to reboot development, and that is to reassert the public interest because it alone takes a long-term view and can guarantee the existence of profit itself.

With policy aiming at the fullest possible employment, profit still has an important role but it is no longer the centre of the economy. In industrial society everything revolved around the production of profit. Work in the public sphere, culture, education and training, and even leisure activities are important only insofar as they contribute to the production of profit, directly or indirectly. In the post-industrial economy, by contrast, increase in productivity comes more from the general growth of society than from specific investment aiming at profit,[34] as Marx himself had foreseen.[35] This is why non-profit work is becoming increasingly widespread and should be encouraged; it satisfies needs that the profit criterion cannot satisfy, especially in the field of personal services and education.[36]

This approach is close to the Commons (common assets) philosophy. These, according to the theoreticians, should be available for use without costs and should include, besides health and education, also housing, public transport, Internet and even Big Data.[37] On the other hand, the EU asserts the need for governments to rewrite the rules for enterprises, obliging them to take charge of the environmental pollution they cause and to take on social responsibility. Governments are to encourage the diversification of forms of ownership and management of firms, including cooperatives, varied ranges of shareholders, and so on.[38]

In this perspective the need—as stressed by Oxfam (2019)—is to guarantee the essential services, which should therefore be public and free,

[33] In 2019 *Social Europe* published many articles arguing that the EU should place employment at the centre of its economic strategy.

[34] See Goodwin (2018).

[35] Marx, *Capital III*, ch. 48, section 13. —*Grundrisse*, notebook VII: 704–706.

[36] See e.g. Sapelli (2018, III.2: 129–134).

[37] Hickel (2019). Ernst (2019).

[38] *Sustainable Equality* (2018, ch. 4).

even in the poor countries, and particularly in the spheres of education and health. These public services are fundamental for development today, as indeed they proved for the development of Western Europe. Funding for the public services and large-scale investments should come from taxation on the highest incomes, policies to fight tax evasion and action against the illegal economy.

It is also necessary to curb the tendency of capitalism to concentrate production in big oligopolies. For example, small-scale agricultural production in the poor countries—Africa, Latin America, India, etc.—has come in for wholesale destruction through the dumping of the rich countries' agricultural produce, enjoying state subsidies. This has led to unemployment and famine in vast areas. There is also an urgent need to stop the agricultural multinationals from exploiting patents to privatise traditional processing techniques and claiming monopoly of seed.

8.3.3 *The Green New Deal*

Many authors see degrowth as the way to curb global warming and restore the polluted environment. This, however, should be so drastic (as even its advocates admit)[39] that it would destroy almost all the existing jobs. The need is, rather, to explore the use of new materials, adopting new techniques and new ways of organising production and consumption. The EU Report on these issues can be seen as an appreciable attempt to organise a new type of sustainable development.[40] Here, too, the institutions must play their part; bottom-up control, as called for by Richard Smith (2015), cannot suffice.

However, an area calling for specific degrowth is that of repetitive goods. These goods are of scant social utility and poor in profit. A part of the workers in this area should be employed in other lines of production, and more specifically those that satisfy the new needs—for example, enhancement of the traditional infrastructures (public transport, hydrogeological remediation, health and educational facilities, restoration of public buildings, etc.)—and creation of new types of infrastructure for mass transmission and digital communications.

The Green New Deal is incompatible with the corporative alliance between entrepreneurs and workers in the old industrial enterprises, which

[39] E.g. Trainer and Alexander (2019).

[40] *Sustainable Equality* (2018).

are high in pollution and low in production. Today, as a result of occupational blackmail, the state is often compelled to pay out for the hidden unemployment lurking in the big industrial aggregates with hundreds of medium-to-low-skilled workers.

With this approach the widespread thesis that environmental remediation boosts employment and can solve the economic crisis makes sense.[41] This can also come about in the sectors of manufacturing and energy.[42] A serious environmental remediation policy calls for specific research in a great many areas, as well as drastic conversion in the direction of non-polluting, resource-saving techniques and detailed regulations for enterprises on the use and disposal of materials.[43] It also calls for painstaking study of ways to guarantee new employment for the workers left redundant by the changes in production.[44] For example, Rifkin observes that the costs of clean energy sources are rapidly falling. They already cost less than fossil fuel. We can now look forward to widespread use of electricity derived from renewable sources, and the possibility of accumulating and selling it, also by private concerns.[45]

A ban must also be brought in on the production of non-recyclable plastics (amounting to at least 30%) and the use of disposable plastic items, as well as strict limitations to the use of chemical pesticides and fertilisers,[46] and indeed factory farming. Taxation should be applied to limit the consumption of meat, which is excessive (45% of farmland is taken up by stock farming), while the law on packaging should be modified to make the various materials easily separable (for differentiated disposal). The cost of drinking water should be raised when used for other purposes, reforestation implemented and effective pressure brought to bear against the destruction of the great tropical forests. And the list could go on, with promotion of electric automobiles, and so on.

Alongside substitution of polluting consumption, there is enormous scope for antipollution activities, and campaigns to educate both firms and consumers in the use of materials and disposal of them. Obviously, there can be no stopping the poor countries from building roads, erecting

[41] See e.g. Aglietta (2014, ch. 9). Holland (2019). Gallagher and Kozul-Wright [2019].

[42] See Eurofound (2019: 9–15). Storrie (2019).

[43] See iASES (2019, ch. 3).

[44] To appreciate the complexity of this issue, see e.g. Galgóczi (2019) on decarbonisation of motive power.

[45] Rifkin (2014: 112–122, 287–296).

[46] See PAN Europe (2017).

buildings and setting up industries. But, with the help of the rich countries, these structures should be created with the new technologies that drastically reduce environmental impact.

8.3.4 A Marshall Plan for the Developing Countries

Nevertheless, if all the investments necessary for the new needs and environmental remediation were implemented, it would be hard to absorb all the unemployment produced by the digital revolution, the relocation abroad of western industry and the reduction of repetitive goods. Hence the need arises to add an enormous field of investment in human capital. *The Western countries will be able to relaunch their own development only if they support development in the poor countries.* To begin with, obviously, the Western countries should put an end to centuries of grabbing from the poor countries, and stop the multinationals from going on with it. So far, despite the pretence of aid, they have failed to do so.[47]

The need is to follow rationale similar to that of the Marshall Plan (on the lips of everybody, but not always appropriately) implemented by the USA in the post-war period. At the time, a huge quantity of staple goods was transferred to Europe or produced in situ thanks to facilitated American loans. The plan proved essential for Europe's economic recovery, but also advantageous for the USA. In the short run, it provided jobs for millions of unemployed American veterans, while in the medium-long period it gave a huge boost to American exports. In the USA, although nothing like a real welfare state was set up, from 1950 to 1970 the income of the 20% poorest households doubled, from $13,000 to $27,000.[48]

Of course, the whole context is very different today. The new plan for development should benefit young people both in the West and in the backward countries. For the latter work, study, training and planning should be carried out partly in the Western countries and partly in the developing countries (a powerful boost for development also comes from the emigrants' remittances as they send part of their earnings home).[49] The employment opportunities would be enormous on both sides.

Just to have an idea, think of the dissemination of agricultural techniques, canalisation of water, the fight against desertification, the

[47] See also Vaggi (2018, ch. 6).
[48] Koo (2016: 22), 2014 value.
[49] See Bonciani (2017).

marketing of the products, and the creation of physical and communication infrastructures. The range is potentially vast, from urban renewal and the organisation and management of refuse disposal and recycling to education in human and civil rights, the rights of women and birth control. Then we might consider action against civil wars (peacekeeping), creation and enhancement of administrative structures, and the fight against corruption. Of course, industrialisation is necessary provided it is, as far as possible, non-polluting. But what is most necessary is growth of human capital and education at all levels. And again, the list could go on.

This is probably the last chance West has to put a stop to its decline and relaunch development. This may seem to call for an economically unsustainable effort, and it certainly will turn out to be so if we leave things as they are, with all the monstrous inequalities, the hoarding of parasitic private wealth and the poverty of the state budgets. But it is worth bearing in mind that many thousands of young people in the West have already found work in the NGOs thanks to the voluntary contributions of millions of citizens. And millions more young people can find work with the support of the states.

Above all, let us not lose sight of the fact that the cost of not implementing a new Marshall Plan would be far higher than the cost of implementing it. Suffice it to consider the economic, political and cultural disasters being caused by the failure to get to grips with the issue of immigration. The price of not launching something like a Marshall Plan is, ultimately, the very existence of our well-being and our civilisation. To save both, we must gradually include the poor countries of the world into well-being, precisely as has been done over the centuries with the underprivileged classes in our countries. This is, in fact, the process that has made it possible for capitalistic accumulation to go ahead so far.

References

Aglietta, Michel (2014) *Europe. Sortir de la crise et inventer l'avenir*, Paris: Michalon.

Benchmarking Working Europe 2019, online, Brussels: European Trade Union Institute.

Bonciani, Barbara (2017) *Rimesse dei migranti e processi di sviluppo*, Milano: Franco Angeli.

Castronovo, Valerio (2011) *Il capitalismo ibrido*, Roma – Bari: Laterza.

Coulter, Steve (2019) "Restoring Trust in Europe – Wage Rises and Workplace Democracy", *Social Europe,* 27th March.

Credit Suisse (2019) *Global Wealth Report*, online.
Deaton, Angus (2013) *The Great Escape. Health, Wealth and the Origins of Inequality*. Princeton and Oxford: Princeton University Press.
Donou-Adonsou, Ficawoyi (2018) "On the Importance of Chinese Investment in Africa", *Review of Development Finance*, 8: 63–73, online.
Ernst, Ekkehard (2019) "Big Data and Its Enclosure of the Commons", *Social Europe*, 12th June.
Eurofound (2019), *Energy Scenario: Employment Implications of the Paris Climate Agreement*, Luxembourg: European Union.
Eurostat, Population & Health (2019).
FAO (2019) Food and Agricultural Organization, *The State of Food Security and Nutrition in the World*, online.
Galgóczi, Béla ed., (2019). *Towards a Just Transition: Coal, Cars and the World of Work*. Brussels: ETUI (European Trade Union), online.
Gallagher, Kevin and Kozul-Wright, Richard (2019) *A New Multilateralism for Shared Prosperity. Geneva Principles for a Global Green New Deal*, UNCTAD & Global Dev. Policy Center (Boston Univ.), online.
Goodwin, Neva (2018) "There Is More Than One Economy", *Real-World Economics Review*, 84: 16–35.
Hickel, Jason (2019) "Degrowth: A Theory of Radical Abundance", *Real-World Economics Review*, 87: 54–68.
Holland, Stuart (2019) "Where the 'Piketty plan' Is Mistaken", *Social Europe*, 28th February.
iASES (independent Annual Sustainable Economy Survey (2019) *The Imperative of Sustainability*, online.
Komlos, John (2018) "Employment in a Just Economy", *Real-World Economics Review*, no. 83: 87–98.
Koo, Richard (2016) "The Other Half of Macroeconomics and the Three Stages of Economic Development", *Real-World Economics Review*, No. 75, June 2016: 2–48.
Madi, Maria Alejandra (2017) "Global Business Models and Labour Challenges", in Garson Lima - M.A. Madi eds., *Capital and Justice*, Bristol UK, World Economic Association: 153–173.
Marx, Karl, *Grundrisse*, trans. from German, written in 1857–61, Harmondsworth: Penguin, 1973.
——— *Capital III* [1863–83], trans. from German, first ed. 1894, New York: International Publishers, online: marxists.org, 1999.
Moe, Espen (2007) *Governance, Growth and Global Leadership*. London and New York: Routledge, 2016.
Moyo, Dambisa (2009) *La carità che uccide*, trans. from English, Milano: Rizzoli, 2010.
——— (2012) *Winner Take All*, New York: Basic Books.

OWD (Our World in Data), ed. Max Roser, online: https://ourworldindata.org/
Oxfam (2019) "Oxfam Briefing Paper", January 2019, Italian version, online.
PAN Europe (Pesticide Action Network Europe) (2017) *Alternative Methods in Weed Management* ..., Brussels, online.
Piketty, Thomas (2014) *Capital in the Twenty-First Century*. Cambridge MA and London: Harvard University Press, trans. from French ed. (2013) and updated.
Piketty, Thomas and Vauchez, Antoine (2018) *Manifesto for the Democratization of Europe*, *Social Europe*, 10th December.
Pollin, Robert (2012) *Back to Full Employment*, Cambridge, MA: MIT Press.
Rifkin, Jeremy (2014) *La società a costo marginale zero*, trans. from English, Milano: Mondadori, 2014.
Salazar-Xirinachs, José M., Peters, E. Dussel, Armony, A., eds. (2019) *Efectos de China en la cantidad y calidad del empleo en América Latina*, Organización Internacional del Trabajo, online.
Sapelli, Giulio (2018) *Oltre il capitalismo*, Milano: Guerini.
Smith, Richard (2015) *Green Capitalism. The God That Failed*, World Economic Association, online.
——— (2017) "China's Drivers and Planetary Ecological Collapse", *Real-World Economic Review*, n° 82: 2–28.
Storrie, Donald (2019) "The Future of Manufacturing. Is It in Europe?", *Social Europe*, 11th April.
Sustainable Equality (2018) Report of the EU Independent Commission for Sustainable Equality, online.
Trainer, Ted and Alexander, Samuel (2019) "The Simpler Way: Envisioning a Sustainable Society in an Age of Limits", *Real-World Economics Review*, 87: 247–260.
Vaggi, Gianni (2018) *Development*, Palgrave Macmillan, Pivot.
Vanhercke, Bart, D. Hailani, S. Sabato eds. (2018) *Social policy in the EU: state of play 2018*, ETUI-OSE: Brussels.

CHAPTER 9

Conclusions: Beyond the Borders

Abstract As human beings grouped together they invented borders to separate themselves from the other groups. Exclusion of the other has always been a way to construct own identity. Progress towards civilisation runs on an interweaving of cultural conquests and conflicts. Today, however, borders no longer function as means to construct identity. We have come to a crossroads: either we go back to barbarism or we break down the identarian borders and recognise the other as a human being, without further qualification.

Keywords Social borders • Self-identity • Xenophobia • Human rights • Conflict

When, in the 1980s, Margaret Thatcher said "there's no such thing as society, there are individual men and women", she thought she was extolling capitalism, or in other words private enterprise. Actually, she was pointing up the crisis of capitalism as social progress, and with it the beginning of a new phase of selfishness—that of neoliberalism—based more on rents than on entrepreneurial initiative. Capitalism had given rise to respect for the citizens and their rights; respect for standards as a form of social

This page is partly inspired by my article in *Sviluppo Felice* and the *Quotidiano di Puglia* of 3/6/2019.

© The Author(s) 2020

C. Perrotta, *Is Capitalism Still Progressive?*,
https://doi.org/10.1007/978-3-030-48169-8_9

solidarity, and human rights to be enjoyed by all, with no discrimination. Moreover, capitalistic accumulation involved a succession of new classes in enjoyment of the wealth produced. Essentially, Thatcher was denying these aspects of capitalistic solidarity.

At the same time, however, any form of solidarity among human groupings has always been experienced together with a contrary element, namely exclusion of the others. From the very outset, human beings have delimited their groupings, practices and values (division of labour, satisfaction of needs, solidarity and trust, duties and rights). This delimitation generated friend-enemy tension between the insiders (family, clan, tribe, nation, religion, political party, etc.) and the outsiders. In fact, as the jurists explain, the very origin of rights lies solely within delimited territories or specific populations, excluding everything outside. On the basis of this exclusion, for example, the Europeans have discriminated against and oppressed other populations. A sense of belonging and a collective identity are necessary for the survival of communities. And yet, it is precisely the other, the stranger, who defines—by contrast—our identity.

However, the identitarian border is not fixed. All sorts of processes are constantly breaking down the old borders to create new ones. Shifting populations, the formation of states or empires, colonisation and conquest of new markets are all phenomena that play a part in destroying borders and reconstructing them along new lines. Obviously, within one and the same community, defined by exclusion of the others, further internal borders are raised (by classes, castes and various forms of groupings), which ceaselessly generate differences, mechanisms of privilege and oppression, discrimination and inequalities. This is our history, consisting in material advances achieved provided some were excluded from them, and cultural progress achieved at the cost of oppression and aggression against others. Today, however, we seem to have come to a radical point of crisis in this dialectic, both human and inhuman. The massive migrations towards the rich countries of the world are the most evident sign of this crisis.

Economic progress has led to the globalisation of trade and communication, but even globalisation is based on exclusion. It has advanced the emerging countries but further impoverished the poorer countries. In the rich countries, it has meant further advance for the classes enjoying guarantees and protection, but it has aggravated the poverty and unemployment of the weaker classes. Globalisation has led to aggressive deployments of wealth and knowledge, and scandalous inequalities. It is driving the young of the poor countries away from their lands—with internal wars, uncontrolled violence, desertification, land-grabbing, destruction of the local economy through dumping and plundering of resources—and, inevitably, towards the rich countries.

In this state of affairs, the working classes of the West are easy prey for the charlatans who point their finger at the migrants as cause of all their ills, as a lever to exploit them all the better and take advantage of them for their own political purposes. Alone and afraid, lacking steady jobs and critical culture, the weaker classes vent their resentment against the false enemies, on the other side of the border. They fail to realise that the real enemy had always been there: the privileged who oppose all attempts at redistribution of wealth—even the mildest and most duty-bound, like paying taxes—and stir them up against the immigrants to protect their own privileges.

This violent—and impossible—endeavour to recover the old identity may mean that, thanks precisely to globalisation, dominating the people is no longer a matter of fixing borders. The choice is either to accept return to the tribal borders or to recognise “the other” as our equal, as a man or woman with the same rights and duties.

* * *

9.1 Addition (April 8, 2020)

The peer reviewer of this book suggested I might add something about the ongoing pandemic: does it in some way change the picture traced out in the book? It seems to me that it not only confirms it, but makes it even more dramatic. The pandemic is unsparingly exposing the acutely severe distortions of today’s economy.

It is becoming all too clear that the present development is not based on increasing social wealth but on rising profits. Whatever the dominant economic theory may have to say, they are in fact two different things. The accumulation of wealth comes from two sources, not one, both impossible to eliminate or reduce to one and the same element. On the one hand, we have private investment aiming at profit, and on the other hand social capital and human capital, which are the constituent elements of society and represent the humus for growth in both production and consumption. If accumulation is reduced to a single factor (profit), then even investment that destroys wealth is interpreted as increasing wealth. For example, production that pollutes the environment boosts profit but in the long run erodes social wealth.

Generating an enormous increase in productivity, industrial capitalism has created well-being for the middle classes of the West, which have burgeoned. Today it is also creating well-being for the middle classes of the emerging countries, which still account for a relatively small proportion of the population but are growing. At the same time, the less protected classes are increasingly prey to unemployment and poverty. We have already seen the reasons for this: delocalisation of western manufacturing without parallel increase in the post-industrial economy, the unregulated digital economy, and deterioration of public services and common goods.

The pandemic has in particular exposed the dire consequences of cutting back on public services (as imposed by austerity policies). As from the creation of the welfare state, a major part of the well-being enjoyed by the lower-to-middle classes has consisted in efficient public services—not only housing, education, health and pensions, but also transport and infrastructures, public administration, socialisation and protection for the weaker classes, as well as vocational training and inclusion in the labour market.

Dismantlement of the public structures—in particular, but not only, in terms of health—has meant a huge boost to circulation of the virus. But it has also been the primary source of poverty and unemployment. This has come about to the advantage of private enterprises performing the same functions, almost always with the financial support of the state (so much for the fervently heralded triumph of the market). And the result can be seen in declining services and, in general, far weaker social efficiency. As might have been expected, this has also harmed the production of profit.

All this adds up to a seriously worsening state of affairs: the new unemployed and poor in the West are not—as once they were—remnants from the past, but come largely from the ruination of the middle classes, and above all of the new middle classes and their children. This is not a passing change, but structural, reversing the historical process of accumulation. For a good thousand years—despite all the negative vicissitudes—the historical process consisted in progressive extension of well-being to the new lower classes. Now it has gone into reverse.

But there is also another, decisive feature of this general deterioration. The proliferation of middle classes in the emerging countries and universal propagation of the Western lifestyle have brought the unlimited destruction of natural resources through production and consumption to the point of unsustainability. With capitalism there has always been the idea that the natural resources are practically unlimited, absurd, of course, but it had seemed almost reasonable as long as the resources were being squandered by a limited minority (the middle-upper classes of the West). When these classes spread and, moreover, saw the addition of the middle classes of the emerging countries, the waste of resources became unsustainable.

With rapid, uncontrolled increase in production and consumption, the environment has been systematically laid waste. The shrinking of the non-anthropized habitat has continued apace. The basic means of survival (water, air, earth, flora, foodstuffs, oceans) have been polluted, and often poisoned. Many animal and vegetal species are being destroyed, often together with tribes of native humans. So it is that the wild animals and their viruses seek survival in the anthropized environment, the latter finding ideal vehicles for circulation in the animals of the mega-farms.

These animals are weakened by the antibiotics, hormones and pesticides they are stuffed with, and enfeebled by the unnatural, tormenting conditions forced upon them. Thus they are easy prey for the viruses, which they pass on to humans. Consumption of meat has taken on a key role in the spread of contagion, partly because it is still—above all in the emerging countries—a status symbol attesting to identification with the middle class.

To the neoliberal way of thinking, then, not only is there "no such thing as society", but, from the economic point of view, there is no such thing even as nature itself. As long as the mega-farms and destruction of Amazonia yield profits, they see no threat to the production of wealth. But then the pandemic jolts us back into recognition that this is simply not true. Systematic poisoning of the environment not only entails the death of millions of humans every year—due to cancer, amyotrophic lateral sclerosis (ALS) or asthma, or to increasingly uncontrollable climate change—but is exposing us ever more to epidemics that kill millions more people, destroy our productive fabric and severely compromise our chances of leading a normal life. Is this the wealth we have produced?

In conclusion it is worthwhile to quote Joseph Stiglitz who—in an article titled "Progressive Capitalism Is Not an Oxymoron"—wrote about "a society that lauds the pursuit of profits as leading, to quote Adam Smith, 'as if by an invisible hand,' to the well-being of society, with no regard to whether those profits derive from exploitation or wealth creation".[1]

[1] In *The New York Times*, April 19, 2019.

Index[1]

[1] Note: Page numbers followed by 'n' refer to notes.

© The Author(s) 2020

C. Perrotta, *Is Capitalism Still Progressive?*,
https://doi.org/10.1007/978-3-030-48169-8

The manufacturer's authorised representative in the EU is Springer Nature Customer Service Centre GmbH, Europaplatz 3, 69115 Heidelberg, Germany. If you have any concerns regarding our products, please contact ProductSafety@springernature.com

Printed and bound by CPI Group (UK) Ltd, Croydon, CR0 4YY
05/10/2026
02228154-0002